MORITZ TILING

HISTORY

OF

The German Element in Texas

FROM 1820-1850

AND

HISTORICAL SKETCHES OF THE GERMAN TEXAS SINGERS' LEAGUE AND HOUSTON TURNVEREIN

FROM 1853-1913

BY
MORITZ TILING
Instructor in History, Houston Academy

FIRST EDITION

Published by MORITZ TILING, Houston, Texas
Nineteen Hundred and Thirteen

Notice

In many older books, foxing (or discoloration) occurs and, in some instances, print lightens with wear and age. Reprinted books, such as this, often duplicate these flaws, notwithstanding efforts to reduce or eliminate them. The pages of this reprint have been digitally enhanced and, where possible, the flaws eliminated in order to provide clarity of content and a pleasant reading experience.

Copyright © 1913 by Moritz Tiling

Originally published:
Houston: 1913

Reprinted:
Janaway Publishing, Inc.
2010, 2013

Janaway Publishing, Inc.
732 Kelsey Ct.
Santa Maria, California 93454
(805) 925-1038
www.janawaygenealogy.com

ISBN: 978-1-59641-210-1

Made in the United States of America

PREFACE.

This plain, unpretending monograph has been written for the purpose of preserving to posterity the records of German achievements in the colonization and upbuilding of the great state of Texas. The pioneer's humble life and courageous struggles are very often left unnoticed by the historian, yet, without his brave and patient labors none of the great commonwealths of the United States would exist. The early pioneer, whose brawny arm wielded the axe, who cleared the forest and broke the virgin soil, is as much a maker of a country, as the statesman, the diplomatist and the soldier of today. His faithful work and often hazardous task are well worth remembering.

The different Texas histories used in the public schools unfortunately are lamentably deficient with respect to the important part the Germans have taken in the colonization and shaping of Texas. Some of them, which are used extensively in the schools of the State, do not make any mention at all of the German immigration and its bearing on the rapid development of Texas, while others at least state briefly that—"Texas is indebted to her German tillers of the soil for developments of great value, and which to Americans had been considered of impossible production in this climate." (Brown's School History of Texas, p. 218.) Prof. A. B. Faust of Cornell University devotes but ten pages to Texas in his History of the German Element in the United States.

Thus the present generation is even now almost ignorant of the men, who went intrepidly into an unknown country, who fearlessly braved the many dangers and hardships incident to pioneer-life and who helped to lay the foundation of the great State of Texas.

The publication of this unassuming book shall remedy this deficiency with proper accounts of the colonization of Texas and will give credit to whom credit is due.

To Prof. C. W. Welch I am indebted for proof-reading and other valuable suggestions.

Houston, Texas.   M. T.

INDEX

Introduction	1-2
Texas Before 1820	3-5
The Immigration Proper Begins (1820-1830)	5-6
German Immigration from 1820-1830	7-11
German Immigration from 1830-1840	12-16
First German Settlement in Texas	17-23
Robert Kleberg, the Founder of Cat Spring	24-29
Cause of the Texas Revolution	30-32
The War for Independence	33-38
The Battle of San Jacinto	39-42
The Immigration Increases After Texas Wins Her Freedom	43-47
First German Societies of Texas	48-52
The Germans in the Republic of Texas	53-57
The Society of German Noblemen	58-62
The Adelsverein Buys a Worthless Land Grant	63-72
Colonization Under the Auspices of the Adelsverein	73-78
Further German Immigration Under the Adelsverein in 1845	79-85
Arrival of More Than 5,000 German Immigrants in 1845-46	86-90
Last Effort of the Adelsverein in Colonization	91-94
Expedition of von Meusebach to the Comanche Territory and His Treaty With the Indians	95-107
Collapse of the Adelsverein	108-113
Criticism of the Adelsverein	114-120
The Revolution of 1848 and Its Effects on German Immigration	121-126
Industrial Establishments of the Early German Settlers and Their Relation to the Anglo-Saxons	127-131
Houston Saengerbund (Display Page)	132
Brief History of the German State Saengerbund of Texas	135-159
Historical Sketch of the Houston Turnverein	161-175
German Day Celebration in Houston	177-181
Works for Bibliographical References	183-185
Landing in Galveston (Poem)	187-189
Die Landreise nach der nuen Colonie (Poem)	189-192
Das Lager auf der Zinkenburg, wo jetzt die Katholische Kirche steht, 1845 (Poem)	192-194
Die erste Ansiedelung der Stadt Neu Braunfels, 1845 (Poem)	194-196
Appendixes	197-225

TEXAS ODE FOR DEDICATION OF THE RICE INSTITUTE
HOUSTON, TEXAS
OCTOBER 12, MCMXII

By Henry Van Dyke.

(In writing this poem Professor Van Dyke made use of an Indian legend. The legend is that when the Indian hears the bees in the forest he knows that his tribe must move on, for the whites are near. He lays stress upon the fact that when the white man brings his women, his children and his bees, he never retreats. It is then that he comes to stay.)

All along the Brazos River,
All along the Colorado,
In the valleys and the lowlands
Where the trees were tall and stately,
In the rich and rolling meadows
Where the grass was full of wild-flowers,
Came a humming and a buzzing,
Came the murmur of a going
To and fro among the tree-tops,
Far and wide across the meadows.
And the red-men in their tepees
Smoked their pipes of clay and listened.
"What is this?" they asked in wonder;
"Who can give the sound a meaning?
Who can understand the language
Of a going in the tree-tops?"
Then the wisest of the Tejas
Laid his pipe aside and answered:
"O my brothers, these are people,
Very little, winged people,
Countless, busy, banded people,
Coming humming through the timber!
These are tribes of bees, united
By a single aim and purpose,
To possess the Tejas' country,
Gather harvest from the prairies,

TEXAS ODE

Store their wealth among the timber.
These are hive and honeymakers,
Sent by Manito to warn us
That the white men now are coming,
With their women and their children!
Not the fiery filibusters
Passing wildly in a moment,
Like a flame across the prairies,
Like a whirlwind through the forest,
Leaving empty lands behind them!
Not the Mexicans and Spaniards,
Indolent and proud hidalgos,
Dwelling in their haciendas.
Dreaming, talking of tomorrow,
While their cattle graze around them,
And their fickle revolutions
Change the rulers, not the people!
Other folk are these who follow
Where the wild-bees come to warn us;
These are hive and honeymakers,
These are busy, banded people,
Roaming far to swarm and settle,
Working every day for harvest,
Fighting hard for peace and order,
Worshiping as queens their women,
Making homes and building cities,
Full of riches and of trouble.
All our hunting-grounds must vanish,
All our lodges fall before them,
All our customs and traditions,
All our happy life of freedom,
Fade away like smoke before them.
Come, my brothers, strike your tepees,
Call your women, load your ponies!
Let us take the trail to westward,
Where the plains are wide and open,

Where the bison-herds are gathered
Waiting for our feathered arrows.
We will live as lived our fathers,
Gleaners of the gifts of nature,
Hunters of the unkept cattle,
Men whose women run to serve them.
If the toiling bees pursue us,
If the white men seek to tame us,
We will fight them off and flee them,
Break their hives and take their honey,
Moving westward, ever westward,
There to live as lived our fathers."
So the red-men drove their ponies,
With the tent-poles trailing after,
Out along the path to sunset,
While along the river valleys
Swarmed the wild-bees, the forerunners.
And the white men, close behind them,
Men of mark from old Missouri,
Men of daring from Kentucky,
Tennessee, Louisiana,
Men of many states and races,
Bringing wives and children with them,
Followed up the wooded valleys,
Spread across the rolling prairies,
Raising homes and reaping harvests.
Rude the toil that tried their patience,
Fierce the fights that proved their courage,
Rough the stone and tough the timber
Out of which they built their order!
Yet they never failed nor faltered,
And the instinct of their swarming
Made them one and kept them working,
Till their toil was crowned with triumph,
And the country of the Tejas
Was the fertile land of Texas.

THE GERMAN ELEMENT IN TEXAS.

CHAPTER I—Introduction.

The brilliant achievements of the conquering hero, the records of marches and counter marches, of skirmishes and battles, of sieges and slaughters, have heretofore been universally accepted as history. This is an erroneous, or at least only partly correct assumption, for such, certainly is not the history of the life and evolution of a people. Neither wars and conquests, nor glittering court life and elaborate social functions, but the quiet, peaceful and productive life of the people is that which makes or unmakes a nation. As Thomas H. Buckle pertinently says: "Nations are great through their architects, engineers, artists, teachers, business men and workers, and not through their lawyers, preachers, soldiers and policemen." The colonization and marvelous development of the United States furnish a striking example of the correctness of this axiom and so does Texas.

A new country is no place for weaklings. Texas, 80 years ago, was such a country in every sense of the word, its broad plains being then the almost undisputed domain of barbarous Indian tribes, whose hunting grounds stretched practically from one end of the great State to the other. It required strong arms and stout hearts to enter this country as a settler and perform the dangerous and onerous work and labor of the pioneer.

The Texas pioneers of the 30s and 40s of the last century—among them more than 15,000 Germans—were such men, who unflinchingly braved all dangers and hardships connected with the arduous task of clearing and cultivating a country that was virtually in possession of ferocious redskins. They fulfilled, as Colonel Roosevelt tersely writes in his book, "African Game Trails," the three prime requisites of any progressive race: "They worked hard; they could fight hard at need, and they had plenty of children." If the Texas pioneers had lacked in any of these essential qualities the Lone Star State would not be, as it is today, dotted with the peaceful homes of more than four million prosperous people.

We of the present generation, living in well organized cities and communities, surrounded by all the comfort and luxury, seemingly indispensable in modern life, can hardly conceive or properly appreciate the hardships and privations of the early Texas pioneer, struggling with the iron difficulties and dangers of frontier life, but we have every reason to hold these men in cherished and revered remembrance. Their noble work should not fall into oblivion.

It is only a little more than four score years since the colonization of Texas, then almost "terra incognita," began. The pioneers of that period are all dead, and of their sons and daughters, the first generation of Germanic blood born on Texas soil, only a few remain to tell their children of the life and the struggles of the early frontiersmen. With the object that the highly interesting records of the important part the Germans took in the colonization of Texas may not be lost and forgotten, this history has been written. The author has been enabled to do this principally through the kind assistance of Prof. Gustave Duvernoy, who for more than 50 years has diligently collected many interesting data and facts connected with the early German colonization in Texas, and who put all this valuable material at his disposal. Other sources of information are the "Texanische Monatshefte," published by the late L. F. Lafrentz, William von Rosenberg's "Kritik des Adelsvereins," and publications by Olmstead, Siemering and Ehrenberg, J. O. Meusebach's "Answers to Interrogatories" and G. G. Benjamin's study, "Germans in Texas."

Texas Before 1820.

There have been a number of conjectures as to the origin of the word Texas. First, That Texas in the language of the aborigines means friends; second, that Tejas, Tecas, or Texas, means tile-roofs, and that the country received that name because some of the Indian tribes lived in houses with tile roofs. Third, that Texas or Tecas means people, and it received that name because inhabited. Fourth, in an article on tribal names of America the National Magazine for August, 1873, said: "The word Techis, from which the word Texas is derived, is a word from the Caddo dialect, and gives title to a population which calls itself Kiwomi, that is, two. The name Tachis or Tecuas was applied to a native confederacy and an ancient province, Ticues, and is said to mean friends, just as Dacotas means allied or leagued." In this last statement there are two facts, viz: First, that the name of Texas was that of an Indian tribe, and second, that this tribe belonged to the Caddo family. Coronado, in 1540, found that tribe on the Red River; he spelled the name Tayos. Joutel, in 1687, found the Tehas, or Taos Indians on the Sabine River. The map of Bellin, published in Paris in 1744, locates the Tchas or Teijas village on the Trinity River. The old maps of Texas of the last century locate the Tehas or Teijas village on the east of the Neches River, at the crossing of the old San Antonio road. It was from that tribe that the name of Texas was derived.

Texas enjoys the unique distinction of having been under six flags. By right of discovery it was claimed by Spain and after LaSalle's expedition (1684-87), by France. When the Spanish colonies in America threw off the unbearable yoke of their mother country (1810-1821), Texas became part of Mexico; from 1836 to 1845 it was an independent republic, then joined the United States as a sovereign State. From 1861 to 1865 the banner of the Confederate States floated over its wide domain, and since then it has prospered again under the Stars and Stripes, having become the Empire State of the great Southwest.

The first attempt at colonization in Texas was made by the well known French explorer, the Chevalier Robert de LaSalle, who entered Matagorda Bay in January, 1685, with three ships, and sailing up the Lavaca River for about six miles, took possession of the country in the name of King Louis XIV. of France, built a fort and a small church and planted crops for the families and the animals and fowls he had brought with him.

Among LaSalle's men was one known as Heins (erroneously spelled Hiens in most Texas histories), who very likely was the first German on Texas soil. This Heins, accompanied LaSalle on his unfortunate expedition for the mouth of the Mississippi River, in January, 1687. When LaSalle was shot by Du Haut, on March 19, 1687, in the camp on the Neches River, this Heins took possession of the valuables, dressed himself in his late chief's uniform and offered himself as leader to the peaceable Nassonite Indians. His further fate is unknown. When two years later (1689) the Spanish Governor of Coahuila reached the place, where LaSalle had built his little fort and church, not a trace of the French men and women left there could be found. All was deserted. Thus ended the first attempt to establish a European settlement in Texas.

The efforts of the Spaniards in colonizing Texas in the eighteenth century were mainly restricted to the building of fortified missions, garrisoned with Spanish troops and inhabited by priests belonging to the Franciscan Order. They tried to Christianize and civilize the Indians, who should then be utilized as a barrier against the coming of foreigners. The success of this policy was rather limited, for the converted Indians generally remained "good" only as long as they were within reach of the Spanish bayonets and rifle balls. On their hunting grounds they were quickly transformed into the ferocious savages of old. The Spanish method of civilizing the Indians proved a dismal failure.

The Immigration Proper Begins—(1820-1830).

Simultaneously with the independence of Mexico (1821) begins the immigration into and the colonization of Texas by the vigorous Teutonic race that was destined to wrest this great domain from the decadent Latin race in 1836 and build up the greatest commonwealth of the United States.

The policy of the Mexican Government in respect to immigration was the opposite of that of the former Spanish authorities. It was comparatively easy for "empresarios" (contractors, or promoters) to receive large land grants from Mexico. The only conditions under which these empresarios received their grants, were that they agreed to pay the cost of survey and recording fees, to bring a certain number of families to Texas within a specified time and to see that none but Catholics should settle in Texas. After the abdication of Emperor Iturbide in 1823, the Mexican colonization law was adopted by the Mexican Congress with the proviso that not more than 11 "Sitios" (one sitio—4428 acres) should ever be granted to one person; viz: One league (sitio) of irrigable land, four leagues of dry, but cultivable land and six leagues of grazing land. This provision was made to prevent land monopolies and on it were based the so-called "11 league claims" in Texas.

The first American empresario securing a claim under this law was Moses Austin, who was born in Durham, Conn., but had spent many years in Missouri, at that time part of the Louisiana Territory. In December, 1820, he arrived at San Antonio and, with the assistance of Baron Von Bastrop, he sent his application for a land grant to Governor General Arredondo at Monterey. His request was granted in January, 1821, but Austin died soon afterward, transferring his grant to his son, Stephen F. Austin, who ably and conscientiously carried out the intentions of his late father.

Among the empresarios of this time were two Germans, Joseph Vehlein and Robert Leftwich (not Leftwick, as spelled in several Texas histories). It seems that Vehlein never made use of his grant and no records exist relating to any land transactions by him. Leftwich's grant dates from the year 1822 and his extensive lands were situated near the old San Antonio road, leading from New Orleans to Texas, between the Colorado and San Marcos Rivers. He built a small fort and settled a few families on his land in 1826, but soon afterward returned to Tennessee, where he formerly had lived, and died there. After his death a company was formed at Nashville in 1830 to carry out the conditions of his contract, but the Mexican Government did not recognize the transfer of Leftwich's claim to this company and gave the land to Austin and S. M. Williams. Four years later the Mexican Government reversed its decision and permitted the Nashville company to succeed as owners of the original Leftwich grant. Thereupon, Sterling C. Robertson brought 500 families from Tennessee and South Carolina as settlers on this fertile land.

CHAPTER II.
German Immigration From 1820-1830.

Texas was first brought to notice of the German people through J. V. Hecke's book, "Reise durch die Vereinigten Staaten" (Travels Through the United States), published in Berlin in 1821. Hecke, a former Prussian army officer, had traveled extensively through the western parts of the United States, and in 1818 had come to Texas, then part of Mexico. He remained in Texas for about one year and after his return to Germany published a glowing report about the beautiful climate, the rich, productive soil and the highly favorable conditions for immigration to Texas. He advised the purchasing and colonizing of Texas by Prussia in the following words: "If there is a land on the trans-Atlantic continent favorable as a colonial possession for Prussia, it is the province of Texas, the acquisition of which by purchase from Spain, to which it is neither of use nor of political advantage, might be very easily made. Certainly very important results in agricultural, political and mercantile respects would accrue from the possession of a country which is greater than Germany. Although at present there is no, or very little, civilized population in that country, in a short time it would become a flourishing colony, if Prussia would make use of the emigrants from Germany who, having become beggars, through the expense of their voyage and lack of employment, suffer wretchedly in the United States. The Prussian Government should furnish them free transportation to Texas on Prussian ships and give them land either gratuitously or grant them support, if only by advanced payments."

He continues that 50 acres (Morgen) of fertile land

would not only be sufficient to support the colonist and his family, but also enable him to pay back in five or ten years all sums advanced to him with good interest, thus becoming an independent land owner.

Urging the purchase of Texas, he writes further: "The sum for which this land might be obtained would not be very heavy, and in case the Government would not desire to furnish the necessary amount, the merchants, who would receive most of the advantage from this colonial possession, might, without difficulty, advance the necessary funds to the State. Then a commercial company, like the British East India Company, might be formed, which should defray all expenses of administration, but also should derive all profits, and the State should only furnish the troops for the protection of the colony against Indian depredations, or any other hostile aggression."

He continues by saying that Prussia could send over 10,000 former soldiers, who could be given land as a gift. With these the colonists could form an effective militia. Prussia's navy would be built up through this colonial possession and Prussia become rich and powerful through its trans-Atlantic commerce.

When we remember that the Monroe doctrine was at that time not yet promulgated and that Iturbide who had just then proclaimed himself Emperor of Mexico, might have been quite willing to part with the province of Texas for a monetary consideration, Hecke's plan of a New Prussia on this side of the Atlantic does not look like an iridescent dream, and leaves a wide field of speculation of what might have occurred, had his ideas been carried out. Quien sabe! As we shall see later, the plan of creating one or more German States in the immense territory west of the Mississippi River, then almost an unknown wilderness, was revived several times in Germany and several unsuccessful efforts were made to realize this idea, that seems preposterous to us, but seemed very probable to many German idealists.

In the fall of the same year in which Hecke's book was published, 53 adventurers of different nationalities landed on Texas soil. This was in the month of October, 1821, the party coming from New Orleans. A report of this expedition in the State archives at Austin contains the following German names: Joseph Dirksen, Eduard Hanstein, Wilhelm Miller, Ernst von Rosenberg, Carl Cuans (?) and Caspar Porton. Nothing definite is known about any of these adventurers except Ernst von Rosenberg. The expedition landed at Indianport (Indianola) and went to La Bahia (Goliad), where, it seems, its members were made prisoners by Mexican soldiers. All participants of this expedition were heavily armed, and the Mexicans, fearing a hostile invasion of Texas, held the adventurers in custody until they received further instructions. Rosenberg was escorted to San Antonio. He had been lieutenant of artillery in Prussia, and when he declared his willingness to join the Mexican army his services were gladly accepted. He received a commission as colonel of a regiment of artillery, and, according to some unconfirmed statements, was shot after the abdication of Iturbide, while, according to others, he fell during the political fights that followed, in battle. A brother of this Ernst von Rosenberg came to Texas in 1849, and his descendants belong to the most prominent German families of Texas of the present time.

The first German colony in Texas was established on the Colorado River, about 30 miles east of the city of Austin. Baron von Bastrop, having received a land grant westward of Stephen Austin's grant, induced a number of German families in the year 1823 to settle on his land on the beautiful banks of the Colorado. (Anton Eikhoff, "In der Neuen Heimat" ("In the New Home," published by E. Steiger, New York, 1885). Nearly all of these pioneer-settlers came from the County of Elmenhorst, Grandduchy of Oldenburg. For 16 years, until the founding of the city of Austin in 1839, this was the farthest northeastern settlement in Texas. Here the sturdy German pioneers, surrounded by ferocious and barbarous Indian tribes, in a wilderness a hundred miles away from civilization, toiled faithfully and undaunted, plowing their fields with guns on their shoulders and performing all the hazardous work incident to pioneer life. When in 1836 Bastrop County was organized, this county comprised all of the present Travis County, and the five commisssioners, appointed by the Texas Congress in 1839 to select a suitable site for a capital of the Republic of Texas, bought 7735 acres in the township of Waterloo, on the banks of the Colorado River, where the city of Austin now stands, for $20,000, the deed for this property being executed by the Sheriff of Bastrop County. It may be of interest to note that when the State agent, John Edwin Waller, and surveyor, W. Sandusky, appointed by President Lamar to survey and plot the grounds purchased for the future capital, arrived at their destination, they found two families, Becker and Harrel, the only inhabitants of Waterloo. Two miles south of Waterloo was another city with the proud name of Montopolis, the rival of Waterloo, also inhabited by two families. On August 1, 1839, Judge Waller sold the first town lots, substantial houses were quickly built, and on October 17 President Lamar with part of his cabinet arrived at the new capitol of the Republic of Texas, received by General Sidney Johnston, Colonel Edward Burleson and Judge Waller, the latter delivering the address of welcome.

The capital of the young Republic grew rapidly, quite a number of Germans taking an active part in the building of the city. Many highly educated men, who had first adopted the strenuous life of the pioneer farmer when they came to Texas from the Fatherland, gradually left their farms for the more congenial life and employment in the city, and the Germans of Austin have forever been a prominent social, political and industrial factor of the capital of Texas.

CHAPTER III.
German Immigration From 1830-1840.

It is highly probable that some German adventurers entered Texas as early as 1800, but no records show their existence. An impenetrable veil is over their fate. A few German settlers came with the colonists brought by Stephen F. Austin and Baron Bastrop, but all we know of them are their names. The first real and productive German immigration to Texas was practically caused by the French July revolution of 1830. This Paris convulsion shook many of the thrones of the petty German princes and threatened for a moment to topple into ruins the whole fabric of absolutism carefully constructed by Prince Metternich at the Vienna Congress. When the storm had subsided and quiet again restored by the liberal use of bayonets and gendarmes, a detestable system of espionage became rampant in many of the German States and principalities. Hundreds of men in all walks of life were put under rigid police surveillance, while many were even imprisoned for expressing or merely holding different political views from those of their governments. The reactionary element was triumphant, while the progressive, liberal minded men were harassed everywhere. Men of education and science, university professors and teachers, jurists and physicians, suffered most from this political persecution. The press was gagged and literary productions subjected to merciless censure.

This deplorable state of affairs naturally created in the hearts of many men of intellect and energy the desire to free themselves in some way from these intolerable political fetters. The revolution, or rather insurrection, having failed, these men were anxious to emigrate to some country with free institutions and a liberal Government, and to found and establish there new homes for themselves and their families under more favorable conditions. Naturally their eyes and thoughts turned westward, where the rising young republic of the United States guaranteed to everybody that freedom of thought and action that had been banished from Europe and especially so from the German States.

During the ten years from 1820-1830 many highly educated Germans, and men of means, had made extensive travels in the United States, west of the Alleghany Mountains, and their letters and reports about that new country proved a veritable revelation to their friends. Many books of travels were published, of which those of Bromme, Gerke, Arends and Duden were the most prominent. The last named, Gottfried Duden, came to America in 1824 and lived for four years in Missouri, then still a wilderness and the most western part of the United States. He returned to Germany in 1828, filled with unbounded admiration for the country he had visited and unlimited enthusiasm for its liberal institutions and Government. His book "Bericht über eine Reise nach westlichen Staaten Nord Amerika's und einen mehrjährigen Aufenthalt am Missouri" (Report of a journey to the Western States of North America and a sojourn of several years on the banks of the Missouri River) was published in 1829 at St. Gallen, Switzerland. The strict censure practiced throughout Germany, would have either eliminated much of its valuable information, thus rendering the book less interesting and useful, or, what is even more probable, might have entirely forbidden its publication.

Duden gives a graphic description of the wonderful country he had visited, of the fertility of the soil, of its vast forests, its extensive prairies, its abundance of fish and game of all kinds, and dwells with great stress on the political, social and religious freedom granted to every settler. He proclaims the land of the Mississippi Valley the new Canaan, the land where millions of the poor and oppressed would find peaceful homes and a comfortable living. In the preface to his book, Duden makes the following caustic but true remarks about the conditions, prevailing at that time in Germany: "The poverty, the administrative coercion, the oppressive financial systems, the tolls and excises, form with us invisibly, and therefore the more dangerous, a kind of serfdom for the common people, which, in some instances, is worse than legally recognized slavery. The puerile idea that one could fill his pockets with gold on the very shores of America has ceased; but one thing is unquestionably guaranteed to the immigrant; a high degree of personal liberty and assurance of comfortable living to an extent that we can not think of in Europe. Millions can find room on the magnificent prairies and valleys of the Mississippi and Missouri, and a nature that has long been waiting for the settler and farmer."

Duden's words fell on open ears and ready minds. The book was read eagerly by thousands of interested men in Switzerland, Baden, Wuerttemberg, Hessen, Rhenish Prussia, Hanover and Oldenburg and had a far-reaching influence. The protracted stagnation of industrial life after the wars of liberation, the unsatisfactory social conditions and, above all, the intensely unpopular system of political reaction, had created among thousands of the higher classes the so-called feeling of being "Europamüde" (tired of Europe). The time for emigration was ripe and Duden's book was the mariner's compass pointing to the proper direction for the burdened and distressed. To the former emigration for economic reasons was now added the emigration influenced by political and romantic ideas. University professors and students alike were fascinated by the plans of creating one or more German States in America with genuine free and popular life, and societies were formed to bring these plans to maturity. Ernest Bruncken in his "German Political Refugees from 1815-

1860" states that the German immigrants of the early 30s came in more or less organized groups. They had more or less definite ideas about establishing States in the United States. These States might or might not be members of the Union, but were to be predominantly German in character. "They would have the Government of the United States itself bilingual, and if the Americans would not grant this—why, then the German States would secede and set up a National Government of their own." (Bruncken, Pol. Ref., Chap. 2.)

For the purpose of furthering this wholesale emigration, societies were formed in different cities of Western Germany, the "Giessener Auswanderungs Gesellschaft" (Emigration Society of Giessen) being the most prominent. G. G. Benjamin in his excellent study, "Germans in Texas," makes the following mention of the objects of this society: "It was organized originally by a number of university men, among whom Carl Follen was the leading spirit. Its aims, as stated in a pamphlet issued in 1833, were: "The founding of a German State, which would of course, have to be a member of the United States, but with maintenance of a form of Government which will assure the continuance of German customs, German language and create a genuine free and popular life." The intention was to occupy an unsettled and unorganized territory "in order that a German republic, a rejuvenated Germany may arise in North America." The members were men of means. Some held high official and professional positions. They sailed in two vessels from Bremen to New Orleans in 1834. After the arrival in this country dissensions arose and the company was broken up. An account of this undertaking is given in Niles' Register and shows clearly what vague ideas existed at that time." (Benjamin's "Germans in Texas," page 6.) While these Utopian plans were never and could never be accomplished, still the western part of the United States gained much by this immigration, and so did Texas, then still part of Mexico. It brought to this country a great number of highly educated and energetic men who not only assimilated themselves readily to existing conditions, but who became the basic element of these embryonic States. It was their hard and persevering labor that opened a vast territory to civilization and made millions of acres productive.

Carl Follen, mentioned above, born at Romrod, Hessen, in 1796, professor at the University of Giessen, is known as the organizer of the Liberal German Students' Societies (Burschenschaften) and prominent political reformer and economist. His many works were a flaming protest against the reactionary system of Metternich, and as early as 1819 he wrote his noted memorial, "Denkschrift über die Deutsche Bildungsanstalt in Nord Amerika" ("Memorial on the German Educational Institute in North America"), in which he developed with great emphasis the establishing of a German University in the United States, pointing out the necessity of such an institution, in order to preserve German customs and ideals in the United States, and especially in the German State, which he believed would be founded somewhere in the Mississippi Valley. Publication of this memorial was forbidden, but a certified copy is to be found in the State archives in Berlin.

Coming to America, Follen lived four years with Duden on his farm in Missouri, then moved to New York and became the first professor of Germanics at Harvard University. He was active in the first slavery agitation, and forever advised the introduction of German athletics (Turnunterricht) in our public schools. He drowned on the high sea in 1840 while being a passenger on a steamer from New York to Boston.

CHAPTER IV.
First German Settlements In Texas.

Among the first Germans who came to Texas must be mentioned Friedrich Ernst and Charles Fordtran, and it is generally assumed that the history of the Germans in Texas begins with the coming of these two pioneers. This was in the year 1831. Ernst, a bookkeeper by profession, was from Varel, Oldenburg, and he, like many others, being dissatisfied with the prevailing conditions in Germany, emigrated with his family to America in 1829, landing in New York, where, for more than a year, he kept a boarding house or hotel. There he became acquainted with Charles Fordtran, a tanner, who was born in Minden, Westphalia, May 7, 1801, and in the spring of 1831 both decided to emigrate to the new State of Missouri. At that time the voyage from New York to the upper Mississippi by water was greatly preferred to the slow and dangerous overland route of 1500 miles.

Ernst, with his family, and Fordtran therefore took passage on a ship sailing from New York to New Orleans, where they arrived in March, 1831. There they heard of the favorable land propositions in Texas, where each married settler was to receive one league and one labor of land (4605 acres) free of charge, and decided to locate in Texas instead of going to Missouri.

On the Mexican schooner Saltillo, Captain Huskin, they arrived in Harrisburg, on Buffalo bayou, on the 3d of April, 1831. After a stay of five weeks at Harrisburg, which then boasted of five or six log houses, they set out to their future new home, a league of land selected by Ernst, where the town of Industry, Austin County, now stands. One-fourth of this league Ernst gave to his companion Fordtran, who also received one league from S. M.

Williams as a compensation for the surveying of two leagues.

While Ernst and Fordtran were not the first Germans coming to Texas, they established the first permanent German settlement there and Mrs. Ernst is universally credited with having been the first German woman in Texas. Ernst and Fordtran built rude log houses on their land several miles apart, but the harmony between them soon ceased. Then Ernst called his place "Industry," while Fordtran's farm received the less inviting name of "Indolence," or "Lazytown," as it was generally called.

Nothing is known of the cause of the disagreement between these two pioneers, but the significance of the names given to the farms leaves room for suggestions as to the origin of the quarrel. Ernst wrote a letter to a friend of his in Oldenburg by the name of Schwarz, informing him about the favorable land conditions in Texas. This letter was published in some newspaper, and through this report several German families were induced to emigrate to Texas. (Full text of this letter in English as translated by G. G. Benjamin, Appendix A.)

Ernst died in 1858, but his widow, who later married a Mr. Stoehr, lived for 57 years at the place where they had settled in 1831. She died at Industry in 1888, at the patriarchal age of 88 years. At the age of 84 years she gave the following graphic description of her family's first years of hardship and privation on their Texas farm: "In New York we had become acquainted with the old rich Mr. J. J. Astor, a stanch and honest German, who advised my husband to start a dairy if he wished to make money. He offered him a 10-acre lot on the East River, where Pearl Street now is, for a few thousand dollars on deferred payments, but although I urged my husband to accept that offer, he refused it, and in April, 1831, we came to Texas, landing at Harrisburg. Houston was then not even known by name, and no ship dared to land at Galveston from fear of the Karankawee Indians (?) who inhabited and infested the island. On ox-carts we traveled 50 miles westward to the town of San Felipe De Austin, where we found one German named Wertzner, among the 300 inhabitants of the place. There we were on the border of civilization. Westward and northward roamed the Indians, and no white man had yet risked to cross the Mill Creek.

"My husband soon set out on an exploring expedition and coming to the forks of Mill Creek, where Industry now stands, he selected a league of land for us, being attracted by the romantic scenery, the pure water, and fine forests around. After having lived in the most primitive style for several months on our new homestead, we sold about one-fourth of our grant, for 10 cows. Now we had at least milk and butter, which was a real Godsend, for the constant monotony of venison and dry cornbread had almost became nauseating. We lived in a miserable little hut, covered with thatch that was not waterproof. We suffered a great deal in winter, as we had no heating stove. Our shoes gave out, and not knowing how to make moccasins, we had to go barefooted.

"For nearly two years we lived alone in this wilderness, but fortunately we were not troubled by the Indians, who were quiet and friendly. In the fall of 1833, some Germans settled in our neighborhood, among them the families of Bartels, Zimmerschreit and Juergens. We naturally hailed their coming with great joy.

In 1834 the following German families arrived here: Amsler, Wolters, Kleberg, von Roeder, Frels, Siebel, Grassmeyer, Biegel and some others whose names I have forgotten. The first settler being killed by Indians was Mr. J. Robinson, the father of Colonel J. Robinson, who lived near Warrentown. In the fall of 1834 the Indians kidnaped and abducted the wife and two children of Mr. Juergens, who had just settled at Post Oak Point, four miles from here. Through the efforts of Father Muldoon, a Catholic Missionary, Mrs. Juergens was returned to her distracted husband, but of the two children, no tidings ever came."

The courage and perseverance of these early German pioneers is worthy of the highest praise. Here they were thousands of miles from their native country, not only in a foreign land, but in the solitude of a wilderness, with dangers of all kinds lurking around them, but unflinchingly did they bear all the numerous inconveniences and hardships incident to pioneer life. Their unreserved love of freedom was the bright star shining above them and guiding them through all the dark hours and troubles of the first years of frontier life, and assisted these intrepid men and women to battle against and finally conquer seemingly insurmountable obstacles.

Ernst's settlement, "Industry," grew rapidly, and for years was one of the most prosperous places in Austin County. It has remained a strictly German town up to the present day, with a thriving and progressive population.

In the years 1832 and 1833 two attempts were made to establish settlements between the lower Nueces River and the Rio Grande. Both were doomed to failure. Johann von Rackwitz, a German nobleman from Wurtemberg, had received a land grant from Mexico in 1832, along the lower Nueces River, and had induced some German families to settle on his land, who had to experience all the hardships and privations of pioneer life in a new country. It seems that Rackwitz was more of an adventurer than an impresario; having no means of his own, he borrowed money from all sources by giving deeds on his lands as security and in 1834 returned to Germany, ostensibly with the intention of bringing back more settlers, but he did not do anything, except to publish a pamphlet at Stuttgart in 1836, entitled, "Kurze und treue Belehrung für deutsche und schweizerische Auswanderer, die an der Begründung der Colonie Johann von Rackwitz theilehmen wollen. (Brief and true instructions to German and Swiss emigrants who wish to participate in the founding of the Colony Johann von Rackwitz in Texas.)

After this he returned to Matamoras where he led a life of dissipation and revelry. No more immigrants arrived and as the conditions of the land grants were not fulfilled, the land escheated to the Mexican Government, everybody who had assisted Rackwitz finally losing everything. The struggling colonists were partly killed and partly fled from their homes, when Santa Anna's army invaded Texas in the spring of 1836.

Another impresario of this time was Dr. Charles Beales of New York, who received an extensive land grant from Mexico on the Lower Rio Grande in 1832. This grant comprised some of the land granted to Joseph Vehlein in 1826, of which the latter had never made any use. The Beales concession bears the date of October 9, 1832. In November, 1833, Dr. Beales sailed with a party of colonists from New York and landed at Copano, on Aransas Bay, at the end of December. The expedition consisted mostly of Irishmen, with only two German families from Bavaria, Schwartz and Wolter, and one single German, Heinrich Taloer, among them. From Copano the party marched through Goliad, then took the old San Antonio de Bexar trail, and, after a slow and toilsome travel, arrived at Las Moras on the "Beales River grant," as it was called, and established the settlement known as La Villa de Dolores in March, 1834.

A second supply of colonists, arriving at Copano in August of the same year, was deterred from going to Dolores by the report started by a settler from Powers' Colony that all the settlers of Dolores had been massacred by the Indians.

In the spring of the year 1835 some more colonists, consisting of three families, five heads of families and 10 single men, reached Dolores. A saw and gristmill were erected and other improvements made. In September, 1835, Dr. Beales returned to New York to bring out colonists who had arrived from Ireland and Germany, but for want of immediate means and other causes, he was delayed there until the spring of 1836, and then the news of the revolution in Texas put an end to all his plans.

The colonists, hearing of Santa Anna's approach, became terror-stricken and dispersed, some going to Matamoras, while others joined the Texans in their fight for liberty and independence. The first attempts of establishing settlements between the Nueces and Rio Grande had failed.

Some Germans, who came to Texas and settled there on land received from the Mexican Government several years before the arrival of Ernst and Fordtran, are mentioned by L. F. Lafrentz in "Texnische Monatshefte," Vol. 11, No. 2, 1906, but nothing is known of most of them except the recording of their land patents in the archives of the general land office at Austin. The first of these pioneers was a German-Swiss named Henry Rueg. He had emigrated to the United States in 1818, and having sufficient means, tried to establish a German colony on the left banks of the Red River in Louisiana. Having failed in this enterprise, he came to Texas in 1821, where he was appointed "jefe politico" (county judge) of Nacogdoches by the Mexican Governor. In Stephen F. Austin's colony the following Germans received land patents: In 1824 Gabriel Strohschneider, whose title was recorded under the name of Gabriel Straw Snider, as he had either Americanized his name in this absurd fashion, or was unable to write. In 1827 two more German names are recorded in the general land office, viz.: Peter Conrad and John Keller, both in Austin's colony, and in 1828 Peter Bertrand. It is very probable that more Germans than those mentioned here were in Austin's colony between 1820 and 1830, but their names can not be identified from the records, because they were either misspelled by the Mexican officials or they changed their names voluntarily to make them sound more harmoniously to Mexican and American ears.

CHAPTER V.
Robert Kleberg, the Founder of Cat Spring.

Among all the Germans that have come to Texas, the family of Robert Kleberg, mentioned above, occupies the first rank. For nearly 80 years members of the Kleberg family have helped to make history in Texas, and it is only fitting in a history of the German element in Texas to make proper account of Robert, Johann, Christian, Justus Kleberg, Sr. Born in Herstelle, Westphalia, on September 10, 1803, he received his education at the gymnasium of Holzminden, and after graduating there, entered the University of Goettingen, where he studied jurisprudence, and received the diploma of doctor juris. After having served in different judicial positions, he, like many others of the best men in Germany, became dissatisfied with the military and administrative despotism, prevalent everywhere, and decided in the year 1834 to emigrate to America. He states his reason for this important change in his life in the following language, taken from a memorandum of his own writing:

"I wished to live under a republican form of Government, with unbounded personal, religious and political liberty, free from the petty tyrannies and the many disadvantages and evils of the old countries. Prussia smarted at that time under an offensive military despotism. I was (and have ever remained) an enthusiastic lover of republican institutions, and I expected to find in Texas, above all other countries, the blessed land of my most fervent hopes."—(Kleberg notes, 1876.)

On September 4, 1834, Kleberg married Miss Rosalia von Roeder, daughter of former Lieutenant Ludwig Anton Siegmund von Roeder, who, too, was anxious to emigrate to Texas with his family. The party had first contemplated going to one of the Western States, but principally through the information gained about Texas from the letter of F. Ernst, it was now determined to go to Texas. His memorandum continues:

"As soon as this was decided, we sent some of our party, three unmarried brothers of my wife, Louis, Albrecht and Joachim, and their sister Valesca, with a servant, ahead of us to Texas for the purpose of selecting a place where we could all meet and begin operations. They were well provided with money, clothing, a light wagon and harness, tools and generally everything necessary to commence a settlement. Six months after our advance party had left, and after we had received news of their safe arrival, we followed on the last day of September, 1834, in the ship Congress, Captain J. Adams."

The emigrants on this ship, all bound for Texas, consisted of the following, viz.: Robert Kleberg and his wife, Lieutenant von Roeder and wife, his daughters, Louise and Caroline; his sons, Rudolph, Otto and Wilhelm von Roeder, Louis Kleberg, Mrs. Otto von Roeder, nee Pauline von Donop, and Miss Antoinette von Donop (afterward wife of Rudolph von Roeder). The other passengers were nearly all from Oldenburg, one of them a brother-in-law of Mr. Ernst, John Reinermann and family, William Frels and others. They were all bound for San Felipe de Austin, and after a voyage of 60 days landed in New Orleans.

To quote further from Kleberg's notes: "Here we heard very bad accounts about Texas, and were advised not to go there, as it was said that Texas was infested with robbers, murderers and ferocious Indians. But we were determined to risk it, and could not afford to disappoint our friends who had preceded us. As soon, therefore, as we succeeded in chartering the schooner Sabine, about two weeks after we had landed in New Orleans, we sailed for Brazoria, Texas. After a voyage of eight days, we were wrecked off Galveston Island, on December 22, 1834. Among the passengers the opinion prevailed that the Sabine was wrecked purposely, in order to get the amount for which she was insured. The wrecked boat was sold at public auction in Brazoria and was bought by a man who had come a few days afterward in the steamer Ocean from New Orleans for $30. It is impossible for me to name with certainty the exact point of the island at which we stranded, but I think it was not far from the center of the island, about 10 miles from the present site of the city of Galveston.

"The island was a perfect wilderness inhabited only by deer, wolves and rattlesnakes. (Kleberg doesn't mention the Indians of which Mrs. Ernst spoke in her interview.) All the passengers were safely brought to shore and were provided with provisions, partly from those on board ship and partly by the game on the island.

"Two or three days after our vessel was beached, the steamer Ocean hove in sight, and observing our distress signal, anchored opposite our camp and sent a boat ashore with an officer to find out the situation. The captain agreed to take a few of us to Brazoria, charging a doubloon ($20) each. I, with Rudolph von Roeder, took passage on it as an agent of the remaining passengers to charter a boat, to take them and their belongings to the main land. Finding no boat at either Brazoria or Bells Landing, the only Texas ports at that time, I proceeded on foot to San Felipe, where I was told I would find a small steamer, the Cuyuga, Captain W. Harris. I found the steamer, but did not succeed in chartering her, the price of $1000 asked being too high.

"In San Felipe I heard for the first time of the whereabouts of my relatives who had preceded us. Here I also made the acquaintance of Colonel Johnson and Captain Moseley Baker, under whose command I afterward fought at the battle of San Jacinto. These gentlemen informed me that my two friends, Louis and Albert von Roeder, had located about 14 miles from San Felipe on a league of land, the present Cat Spring, but that Joachim and Valeska von Roeder had died. I found Louis and Albert in a miserable hut and in a pitiful condition. They were emaciated by disease and want of proper treatment and nourishment. Tears of joy streamed from their eyes when they beheld me and my companion. After a few days of rest I continued my search for a boat. I had a letter of introduction to Stephen F. Austin and Sam Williams from a New Orleans merchant, but both gentlemen were absent from Harrisburg, when I reached there. Fortunately, I succeeded in chartering a small vessel from Mr. Scott, the father of Mrs. Williams, for three trips to Galveston, for $100, and immediately returned to Galveston, landing on the bay side, opposite the camp of the stranded passengers, just four weeks after I had left it. I found all the passengers in good health and spirits. They had spent most of their time in hunting and fishing. Those who could not shoot were employed to drive the deer to the hunters. There were deer by the thousands.

"The next day I left with the first cargo of passengers, including my wife, her parents and Caroline von Roeder. After a stormy trip we arrived in the evening of the same day at Mr. Scott's place, where we were hospitably treated. I was fortunate to find quite a comfortable house in Harrisburg, which I rented, as we intended to remain there until all passengers had arrived from the island.

"The last passengers did not come until the fall of 1835, although I had hired another small sloop from Captain Smith in Velasco, that also made three trips. The winter of 1835 was unusually severe."

Thus ended the lengthy and eventful voyage of some of the earliest German pioneers from the Fatherland to Texas. While only the main incidents are related, they are sufficient to show the difficulties and privations to which Texas emigrants in those early days were subjected. But their troubles were by no means ended. From Harrisburg they had to travel in ox-carts for more than 50 miles over almost impassable roads before they reached their point of destination in Austin County. Then their first task was to erect some houses, but, as Mr. Kleberg writes, "not being accustomed to manual labor, we proceeded very slowly." Fortunately for these settlers the Indian tribe living in their neighborhood, the Kickapoos, were friendly, and of great help to them. They furnished them with game of all kinds and the squaws would hunt and bring into their camp the horses and oxen that had strayed.

Kleberg continues in his notes: "We had supplied ourselves with everything necessary to commence a settlement in a new country. We had wagons, farming implements, all sorts of tools, household and kitchen furniture, and clothing which we had brought with us from Germany. Early in summer, 1835, we had finished building two log houses, one of them had even a floor and a ceiling, having sawed by hand the planks from post oak trees.

"We had also enclosed and planted a field of ten acres in corn and cotton and we now moved the members of our family who had remained in Harrisburg to our settlement. Such of our goods for which we had no room or immediate use, we left at the house we had rented at Harrisburg. Among the objects we left was a fine piano, belonging to my wife, many valuable oil paintings, music, books, etc., all of which fell a prey to the flames, which consumed Harrisburg during the war that followed in the following spring."

This was the beginning of the present town of Cat Spring, Austin County, which up to date has preserved a thoroughly German character. Industry and Cat Spring, Austin County, and Biegel's settlement in Fayette County, founded 1835, were the first pure German settlements in Texas. Baron Bastrop's colony in Bastrop County was established some years previous to these settlements, but most of the colonists there were Americans from the States, only interspersed with some Germans from Oldenburg.

Of the pioneer German settlers in Texas, Robert Kleberg was by far the most prominent and influential. Mention of his eventful career and long and useful life will be made in succeeding chapters. The principles which found expression in his whole life, rested upon a broad and comprehensive philosophy of which absolute honesty and righteousness were a controlling element, and when the shadows of death gathered around him, he met the supreme moment with a mind serene and in peaceful composure.

CHAPTER VI.
Causes of the Texas Revolution.

Anastasia Bustamente, a bigoted, unprincipled military chieftain, had deposed President Guerrero of Mexico in 1829, and had assumed the Presidency. Being a devout Catholic, he wished to exclude further immigration of Protestants from the United States into Texas. Therefore, on April 1, 1831, he issued a decree, the eleventh article of which prohibited further immigration of Americans into Texas. The colonization law of 1824 was repealed and another, based on Bustamente's decree, was passed by the Mexican Congress.

In 1831 Mexican custom houses were established at Nacogdoches, San Antonio, Copano, Velasco and Anahuac. By decree of April 7, 1832, foreigners (meaning Americans) were forbidden to carry on retail trade in the country. To overawe the colonists, a considerable body of Mexican troops was sent into Texas. Colonel Piedras, the ranking officer, had 320 men at Nacogdoches; Colonel Bradburn, 150 at Anahuac; Colonel Ugartechea, 120 at Velasco. Colonel Bean had a small force at Fort Teran, on the Netches, and there were also companies at Tenoxticlan, Goliad and San Antonio. By a military order all ports of Texas, except Anahuac, at the head of Galveston Bay, were closed. The Mexicans soon became very arrogant and annoyed the Texans in every way possible. The commanders shielded their soldiers from punishment, even after their misdemeanors had been clearly proven. They received runaway slaves in their forts and refused to give them up, under the plea that they had already enlisted in the Mexican Army. In the spring of 1832, Bradburn arrested and imprisoned in his fort, without authority of law, a number of the most prominent American citizens for whom he had conceived a dislike. Among these prisoners were William B. Travis, Patrick C. Jack and Samuel T. Allen, who in vain demanded to be informed of the charges against them, and to be tried by civil authorities.

When the Texans heard of this arbitrary act of military despotism, they became furious. Meetings were held and measures devised to effect the release of the prisoners in the stockade. A company was organized under the command of F. W. Johnson, and the immediate and unconditional release of the prisoners was demanded. This company marched against Anahuac, when Bradburn refused to accede to the demand, but at that time Colonel Piedras arrived from Nacogdoches and as soon as he had ascertained the true state of affairs, released the prisoners.

At this juncture, a new revolution in Mexico put Santa Anna in power. He proclaimed anew the constitution of 1824, but the people of Texas were then clamoring for a constitution of their own, and wished Texas to be separated from Coahuila, of which State it was then a part, and have Texas proclaimed a sovereign State. An election was held in the different municipalities in March, 1833, and in April a convention met in San Felipe. A constitution which was drafted by Sam Houston was adopted and submitted to the national authorities for approval. Judge Burnet drew up an able memorial, showing the disadvantages under which Texas labored, and the necessity for a separate State Government, and Stephen F. Austin carried the documents to the City of Mexico. There the political situation had again changed with lightning rapidity. Santa Anna had abandoned the liberal party and was making strides toward an absolute dictatorship. The constitution of 1824 had again been swept away and the mass of the people disarmed. On the 11th of May, 1835, Santa Anna won a complete victory near the City of Mexico over the last Republican leader, Governor Garcia of Zacatecas. The Republic had disappeared and was replaced by a military dictatorship. In October, 1835, Santa Anna issued a decree suspending the functions of all State Legislatures, and centralizing all power in the supreme government at the capital; the end of all State Government was at hand.

At this period, Austin, who had been kept in confinement in Mexico for two years, returned to Texas. The people were anxious for his advice. To secure concerted action, he advised the assembling of delegates from all municipalities for a general consultation. This meeting, after two adjournments, finally took place at San Felipe on November 3, 1835. After much discussion a declaration for a provisional State Government under the Mexican confederacy was adopted on November 7. Many Texans then believed that there existed in Mexico a strong Federal Liberal party, and the declaration was so framed as to invite a co-operation with them in restoring the constitutional government of 1824. But Santa Anna ruled in Mexico with an iron hand and was resolved to punish the Texans for their insolence. By the middle of February, 1836, he was ready to invade Texas in three divisions. The momentous struggle for the independence of Texas began, a struggle during which untold barbarities were committed by the invading Mexican armies and during which the young German settlements on the Colorado River and Mill Creek suffered terribly. Santa Anna seemed determined to destroy all foreign civilization by burning and pillaging all farms through which he came with his troops, but the imminent danger of utter ruin tended greatly to unite the different factions in Texas into a harmonious body for the defense of their adopted country, in which Americans and Germans equally shared.

CHAPTER VII.
The War for Independence.

During the five years from 1831-1836 quite a number of Germans had come to Texas, most of them bringing their families with them. When the conflict with Mexico was inevitable and the call for volunteers was issued by President Burnet of the Provisional Government, the German settlers, true to their democratic character and love of liberty, responded readily. Many had been the privations and severe the task which these early settlers had already undergone, but their trials were far from being ended. The furies of war threatened to devastate their settlements, erected with tender care only a few years before.

After the fall of the Alamo (March 6, 1836) and the subsequent massacre at Goliad (March 27) it was evident that the colonists could expect but scant consideration from Santa Anna and his minions. Two courses were left to them, viz.: Either to abandon their new homes and flee with their families to the United States, or fight for their freedom. Many of the Texas settlers chose the former course. To quote the historian: "The general dismay induced many brave men, impelled irresistibly by natural impulses, to go to their abandoned wives and children to tender them protection. The flight of the wise and worthy men of the country from danger tended to frighten the old, young and helpless, furnished excuses to the timid and sanctioned the course of the cowardly."

Under the direction of Robert Kleberg, the German settlers of Industry and Cat Spring held a meeting to decide whether to fight for Texas independence or to cross her borders into the United States, to seek shelter under the protecting aegis of the American eagle. This council of war was held under the sturdy oaks on the newly acquired possessions. It was a supreme moment in the lives of those who participated. They found themselves in the midst of a terrible panic, and they were now called to decide between love of country and love of self, and it may well be presumed that the debates in this little convention were of a stormy nature. It was principally through the eloquence of the venerable lieutenant, Von Roeder, and Robert Kleberg that the decision was finally reached that the men would remain to share the fate of the heroic few who had rallied under Sam Houston to fight for the independence of Texas against Mexican despotism, while their families should be sent to places of safety. It was a pathetic scene, when these brave men bade good-bye to their wives, who, mounted on Texas ponies, started eastward, driving their cattle and horses before them over the wide prairies, to cross the border of Texas into Louisiana.

The muster rolls of the participants in the war for the independence of Texas in the State archives at Austin contain the following German names: Carl Amsler, Louis Amelung, Jacon Albrecht, William Ahlert, Joseph Biegel, Joh. Burgiesky, Joh. Baumbacher, Thomas Bertram, W. M. Burch, Franz Dietrich, M. Dombriski, Georg Erath, F. G. Elm, Herman Ehrenberg, Conrad Eigenauer, Bernard Eilers, Fritz Ernst, Albert Emanuel, Joseph Ellinger, Carl Fordtran, Carl Felder, Abraham Formann, Peter Fullenweider, Wilhelm Frels, Wilhelm Friedlander, F. W. Grassmeyer, Jacob Geiger, F. Griebenrath, C. Giesecke, J. Herz, Christian Hildebrandt, Moritz Heinrich, G. Herder, Joh. Hollien, Joh. Heunecke, Ed Harkort, J. A. Heiser, F. Heusemann, H. Halt, C. Hammacher, F. Hellmueller, Conrad Jurgens, Thomas Kemp, Louis Kleberg, Robert Kleberg, A. Kinschel, L. Krup, J. Kolmann, Joh. Kopf, L. D. Kessler, F. Keller, L. Kranz, A. Lehmkuhl, G. Luckenhoger, C. Luenenburg, William Langenheim, Charles Lantz, G. Luck, F. Lundt, F. Luders, William Mayer, Peter Mattern, C. Messler, J. Miller, F. Niebling, J. Oberlander, J. Peske, P.

Pieper, W. Preusch, J. Reinhardt, E. Pucholaski, A. C. Redlich. John Reese, G. W. Ricks, Louis v. Roeder, Otto v. Roeder, Rud v. Roeder, Joachim v. Roeder, William v. Roeder, L. Schulz, H. Schultz, J. Schur, A. Stern, A. Stolke, F. Schrack, C. Schultz, F. Schroeder, B. Strunck, G. Sullsbach, H. Thuerwachter, C. Tapps, J. Volkmar, Sam Wolfenberger, William Wagner, Henry Wilke, Phil Weppler, J. Wilhelm, R. Wilhelm, A. Winter, L. v. Zacharias, J. Zekainski, William Zuber.

Most of these brave defenders of Texas fought under Sam Houston, while the following were members of Colonel Fannin's gallant command, that was murdered at Goliad, viz:

In Captain Duval's company, First Regiment Texas Volunteers, William Mayer, J. Volkmar; in Captain Pettus' company, San Antonio Grays, William Preusch, John Reese; in Captain Bullock's company, First Regiment Texas Volunteers, H. Schultz; in Captain Ticknor's company, First Regiment Texas Volunteers, Charles Lantz; in Captain Wyatt's company, Huntsville Volunteers, M. Dombrinski, J. H. Fisher, F. Peterswich; in Captain Burke's company, New Orleans Grays, Jacob Kolmann, Peter Mattern, Hermann Ehrenberg, Conrad Eigenauer, G. Kurtmann, Joseph Spohn, Thomas Kemp; in Captain Shackleford's company, Red Rovers, A. Winter, Robert Finner, J. Heiser, J. Miller, B. Strunck.

Of the 365 men of Fannin's command, only 27 escaped the brutal and unprovoked, cold-blooded murder. Some were saved before the execution by the Mexican Colonel Garay, some were employed as nurses at the hospital, while some escaped by feigning death after the first fusillade. Among the latter was Hermann Ehrenberg of the New Orleans Grays, who a few years after this horrible drama, published his experience in book form, "Texas und seine Revolution" (Texas and Its Revolution) Leipzig, 1843, which contains a graphic description of the surrender of

Fannin to a superior Mexican force, of the seven days' imprisonment of the Texans in the fort at Goliad and their uncalled-for massacre on Palm Sunday. We quote the following: "On the fifth day of our imprisonment all the German captives were called out by Colonel Holzinger of the Mexican artillery, who asked them to enter the Mexican service as artillerymen, but his proposition was disdainfully rejected by all of us. What a shameful suggestion! We should assist to destroy a young Nation fighting for her rights, for her freedom of humanity! 'No,' answered Mattern, our spokesman, 'if you left us the choice between a high office in Mexico or a life of hardship in your mines among your criminals, we should select the latter, before raising one arm in a service for suppression of liberty. No, Colonel, we thank you, but our views differ widely. Our minds are going forward with the times, yours and that of the Mexican Government are marching in the opposite direction. But it is useless, your time is gone, the people know that it is they who have the authority to make laws for their governments.'

"The eighth day of our imprisonment began. A courier from Santa Anna had arrived during the night, bringing, without doubt, the decision of our fate. We were anxiously awaiting the news, to be brought at once to Matamoras or Copano, according to the stipulations of the surrender, to greet again the blue waves of the Gulf of Mexico, to cross its placid waters, and finally to ascend the mighty Mississippi to that city which we had left seven months ago. We would be free.

"To our surprise we noticed that during the night the cannon at the gates had been turned toward our camp in the fort and loaded, for the artillerymen stood beside them with lighted fuse, ready to fire. It was 8 o'clock when an officer stepped toward us reading from Santa Anna's order that we should march off immediately. Whither, was not stated and left to our imagination. In a few minutes we were ready, and, after roll call, we marched in double file through the gloomy gates of the fort, as we believed, to our expected freedom. Outside the gates we were surrounded by Mexican infantry on both sides and silently marched on. But the road we were taking did not lead to either Copano or Matamoras, but to Victoria. Turning around, I noticed to my intense surprise that only a part of us were marching with our column, while the others were taking an opposite direction. We had been separated. What was the purpose of this action? To what place were we marching? After a silent march of a quarter of an hour we turned to the right toward the San Antonio River, and when we reached a mesquite fence running along the beautiful stream, the guard line on our right side fell back and took position behind the one on our left side. Then the unexpected command, 'Halt!' that sounded to us like a death knell, for at that very moment we heard from afar the rumbling sound of a volley of musketry and we instantly thought of our comrades who had been led in that direction. Astonished and frightened, we looked at each other and at the Mexicans, when the second command, 'kneel down,' completely terrified us and at the same instant the Mexican rifles were pointed at our breasts. A second volley from another direction than the first sounded in our ears, then we heard the command, 'fire!' and then—all was still. A thick powder smoke rolled slowly towards the San Antonio River. The blood of my lieutenant was spattered on my clothing, and around me my friends were writhing in agony; beside me lay Kurtmann and Mattern, breathing their last, but I was not wounded. Hastily I rose and, protected by the dense smoke, I rushed toward the river. Pursued by some Mexicans, I dived in the clear waters, shouting, 'The Republic of Texas forever,' and succeeded in reaching the opposite bank, although the Mexicans sent several bullets after me that fortunately missed their mark. After a last look backward, and a parting greeting to my murdered comrades and friends, I hurried through the prairie to a nearby wood, where I was comparatively safe from further pursuit. By a miracle I had been saved from an ignominious death, and now, being under shelter, I fell down to the ground trembling and exhausted."

Ehrenberg, William Langenheim and Joseph Spohn, who had been detailed to hospital service, were the only Germans who escaped the ruthless massacre of Goliad. This cruel and wholesale murder is perhaps the darkest blot of modern history, exposing beyond a shadow of doubt the blood-thirsty and treacherous Mexican character that this decadent Latin race is still possessed of today, despite the civilization of the Twentieth Century.

A history of the early German settlers in Texas would be incomplete without mentioning Squire Adolf Stern, the German justice of Nacogdoches. Stern was commissioned by the Provisional Government of Texas in the fall of 1835 to go to New Orleans in order to appeal for assistance in the coming struggle with Mexico. He very ably fulfilled his mission. He succeeded not only in raising $10,000 from the people of the Crescent City, but also organized three companies of volunteers, the New Orleans Grays, the Mobile Greys and the Tampico Greys, a most valuable addition to the limited fighting force of the Texans. The first of these companies left New Orleans for Texas on October 12, 1835, the second following on the next day. There were seven Germans in these two companies. The Tampico Greys, as their name indicates, went directly to Mexico for an attack of Tampico.

CHAPTER VIII.
The Battle of San Jacinto.

While this book is not a history of Texas and some may believe that special mention of the Battle of San Jacinto be unnecessary, the author is of the opinion that a short description of this momentous affair, in which quite a number of Germans were active participants, will not be amiss.

General Sam Houston, commander in chief of the "Army of Freedom," had slowly retreated before the superior forces of Santa Anna from Gonzales to the mouth of the San Jacinto River, picking up during his retreat all the settlers who wished to join in the defence of Texas liberty. He was closely followed by Santa Anna. On the memorable morning of April 21, he had under his command 783 men, while Santa Anna's force numbered about 1600. About 12 o'clock a. m. a council of officers met in the Texas camp, after which Sam Houston issued the following order to the little band under his command: "Today we are ready to meet Santa Anna. It is the only chance of saving Texas. From time to time I have looked for reinforcements. We will have only 700 men to attack with, besides the camp guard. We go to conquer. It is wisdom growing out of necessity to meet the enemy now. Every consideration enforces it. No previous occasion would justify it. The troops are in the spirit now. It is time for action.

"Sam Houston, Commander in Chief."

With these brave and courageous words still ringing in their ears the heroic little band of Texans was ready for the assault. At the sound of the bugle, about 4 o'clock, the whole Texas line shouted the battle cry, "Remember the Alamo!" "Remember Goliad!" and rushed impetuously upon the foe. The Mexicans at that late hour were not expecting an attack. Many of them were taking their evening "siesta." Before their lines were formed, the Texans had charged over their breastworks, taking their cannon. The Mexicans fled in confusion, leaving their camp and baggage to the victims. With the battle cry: "The Alamo!" and "Goliad!" ringing in the ears of the Texans, there was a fearful slaughter of the foe as long as there was any show of resistance. In less than half an hour the Mexican army was completely routed.

General Sam Houston in his report of the engagement to President Burnet gives the following graphic description of the battle:

"General Sherman and his regiment having commenced the action upon our left wing, the whole line, at the center and on the right, advancing in double quick time, rung out the war cry, 'Remember the Alamo!' received the enemy's fire and advanced within point blank shot before a piece was discharged from our lines. Our line advanced without a halt until they were in possession of the woods and the enemy's breastworks, the right wing of Burleson's and the left wing of Millard's taking possession of the breastwork—our artillery having gallantly charged up to within 70 yards of the enemy's cannon, when it was taken by our troops. The conflict lasted about 18 minutes from the time of close action until we were in possession of the enemy's encampment, taking one piece of cannon (loaded), four stands of colors, all their camp equipage, stores and baggage. Our cavalry had charged and routed that of the enemy upon the right and given pursuit to the fugitives, which did not cease until they arrived at the bridge, which I have mentioned before. Captain Karnes—always among the foremost in danger—commanded the pursuit. The conflict in the breastworks lasted but a few minutes; many of the troops encountered hand to hand, and not having the advantage of bayonets on our side, our riflemen used their pieces as war clubs, breaking many of them off at the breach. The rout commenced at 4:30 and the pursuit by the main army continued until twilight. A guard was then left in charge of the enemy's encampment and our army returned with their killed and wounded, six of whom mortally. The enemy's loss was 630 killed, among whom was one general, four colonels, two lieutenant colonels, five captains and twelve lieutenants. Wounded, 208, of which were five colonels, seven captains and one cadet; prisoners, 730. President General Santa Anna, General Cos, four colonels—aides to General Santa Anna—and the colonel of the Guereo battalion are included in the number. General Santa Anna was not taken until the 22d. General Cos April 21, very few having escaped. About 600 muskets, 300 sabers and 200 pistols have been collected since the action; several hundred mules and horses were taken and near $12,000 in specie. For several days previous to the action our troops were engaged in forced marches, exposed to excessive rains and the additional inconveniences of bad roads, illy supplied with rations and clothing, yet amid every difficulty they bore up with cheerfulness and fortitude and performed their marches with alacrity. There was no murmuring.

"Previous to and during the action my staff evinced every disposition to be useful and were actively engaged in their duties. In the conflict I am assured that they demeaned themselves in such a manner as proved them worthy members of the army of San Jacinto. Colonel T. J. Rusk, Secretary of War, was on the field. For weeks his services had been highly beneficial in our army. In battle he was on the left wing, where Colonel Sherman's command first encountered and drove the enemy; he bore himself gallantly and continued his efforts and activity, remaining with the pursuers until resistance ceased.

"I have the honor of transmitting a list of all the officers and men who were engaged in the action, which I respectfully request may be published as an act of justice to the individuals. For the commanding general to attempt discrimination as to the conduct of those who commanded or those who were commanded, would be impossible. Our success in the action is conclusive proof of much daring, intrepidity and courage; every officer and man proved himself worthy of the cause in which he battled, while the humanity which characterized their conduct after the victory richly entitles them to the admiration and gratitude of their general. Nor should we withhold the tribute of our grateful thanks from that Being who rules the destinies of Nations, and has in times of greatest need enabled us to arrest a powerful invader while devastating our country.

"I have the honor to be, with high consideration, your obedient servant,

"Sam Houston, Commander in Chief."

Of the Germans participating in this glorious battle, special mention deserves to be made of Colonel Eduard Harcort, chief of staff of General Sam Houston. After the victory of San Jacinto he was ordered to quickly construct a fort on Galveston Island for the detention of the Mexican prisoners. There he contracted fever, from the effects of which he died in the fall of the same year that had secured the independence of Texas.

This is the brief history of the battle of San Jacinto, which, insignificant in regard to the numbers engaged, was of the utmost importance in its results. By this victory the independence of Texas was won and the sovereign authority of the Teutonic race over its wide domain was firmly established. The sway of the decadent Latin race over a large part of North America had come to an end and was replaced by the progressive rule of the sturdy, intelligent and industrious Anglo-Germanic people. San Jacinto was the just retribution for the outrages committed by the Mexicans at the storming of the Alamo and for the wanton massacre of Goliad.

CHAPTER IX.
The Immigration Increases After Texas Wins Her Freedom.

When the colonists with their families returned to their former homes, after the precipitate flight of the remnants of the Mexican armies across the Rio Grande, they found their houses burned and their growing crops partly destroyed. But undismayed by their loss, most of these intrepid men set instantly to work to rebuild their old homes, to replant their crops and with undiminished vigor started life anew in their now free adopted country. More immigrants arrived from the Fatherland and new settlements were started. The families von Roeder were the founders of Shelby, Austin County, while William Frels established Frelsburg, the first German settlement in Colorado County. In 1837 the first houses were built on a bluff on the banks of the Colorado River, the beginning of the present city of LaGrange. The land was the property of a Mr. John Moore, who had come from Tennessee with the first settlers of Stephen F. Austin's colony. The next year the plan of the new city was made and platted by Bird Lockhardt, one of the settlers, and Moore waited for the inhabitants of his town to come. He was fortunate. A number of German immigrants who intended to settle in Bexar County were unable to cross the Colorado River on account of high water, which lasted for several months. Moore, hearing of their plight, offered to give to each of the colonists a town lot of 81 by 171 feet, if they would decide to stay there and help him start the new city. They accepted his offer, and thus the city of LaGrange received its German character that has been preserved to the present day.

The arriving and settling of many Germans in Texas from 1836-39 is conclusively proven by the archives of the General Land Office of Texas, which contains the following German land owners that had been recorded up to October, 1839, besides those previously mentioned in this history: Andreas Baldinger, Charles F. Baeumlein, Jacob Blum, Jonathan Buhn, P. Bugler, Bernhard Cerchner, Daniel and J. M. Cruger (Krueger?), John Cruse, Carl F. Dresler, C. C. G. Eberling, C. B. Fanger, Otto Finte, Carl Fledsner, Albert Friedrich, Andreas Gabel, Ferdinand Gerlach, Adolf Glaveck, Gottlieb Gosche, Friedrich Gundermann; G. L. Haas, Conrad Habermehl, John F. Harig, Friedrich Happle, Franz W. Hermes, F. Helfenstein, George A. Holzmann, Christoph Huth, John Janson, Heinrich Kattenborn, William Kieffer, John Kops, Ferdinand Kessler, Philipp Kestler, Jacob Kindig, D. Kerger, Benjamin F. Klein, H. Knapp, Christian and Conrad Knodel, Peter Knoll, John Kohlmann, Henry Kraber, Wilhelm Krisinger, Teodor Leger, Teodor Lehmann, Carl Lunenburg, George W. Lueckenhoger, Henry Lotter, Friedrich Ludwig, Friedrich Lundt, Gustav Loeffler, Samuel Maas, Felix Martel, Heinrich Maurer, Burchard, Friedrich H. and Peter Miller, John B. Moser, Andreas Neuschofer, Henry Orender, Z. M. Paul, Martin Peske, Heinrich Prosius, Heinrich Ratterhorn, Adolf Reiman, Franz Reimar, George Risner, A. C. and L. M. Rothermel, Englebert Ruhl, Martin Mumps, Carl Schaller, Carl Schlicht, Conrad, Martin, Valentin, W. H. and J. H. Schnell, Ferdinand Schroeder, William H. Schrier, F. Seeholzer, F. Siedekum, Thomas Silte, John Solberg, Franz Stadt, Friedrich Steusig, Heinrich Stauffer, Heinrich Stutz, Heinrich Trott, Friedrich Utz, August Wagner, Thomas Weidmann, Joseph Weyl, T. G. Welchmeyer, Kasper Whistler, Joseph Wiehl, Johann Wohler, Carl Wolf, John Wyche, Friedrich von Wrede and Franz Zelner.

During the year 1838 the society "Germania" was organized in New York with the object of establishing a German colony in Texas. Men in all stations of life, professional men, tradespeople and mechanics, joined this society,

German Element in Texas 45

hoping to better their lot in the new country. The conditions then prevailing in the United States were fostering emigration. The hard times and the financial panic that followed the Jacksonian epoch had ruined thousands in all parts of the United States and drove other thousands from the country. The Germania Society sent the first section of emigrants, consisting of 130 people, to Texas in their own brig, North, from New York on November 2. The vessel arrived at Galveston on Christmas Day, 1839. There they heard the unwelcome news that a few days previous the last victim of a yellow fever epidemic, a German, had been buried at Houston, which was almost depopulated. This deterred most of the colonists from disembarking and many returned with their ship and their leader, Dr. Schuessler, to New York. The more courageous remained and went to Houston. Among the families that settled in Houston, then a town only three years old, were the families Usener, Schweickart, Habermehl, Bottler and Karcher, and a single man by the name of Schnell.

Most of the single men from the ship North went to Cat Spring, where they bought lands from the Klebergs. Robert Kleberg, returning to Cat Spring after the battle of San Jacinto, found his house and the outbuildings burned and destroyed and decided to abandon the settlement commenced on the Brazos River and settle on the Island of Galveston on two leagues of land which were chosen there. This enterprise proved a total failure. Kleberg has the following to say about his endeavor to settle on Galveston Island: "We remained about three months on the island after building our house. Most of us were always sick, especially the women and children, long exposure, bad food and water being the probable causes. Not long after we moved into the house, Mrs. Pauline von Roeder, the wife of Otto von Roeder, died there. We were all down with chills and fever. The deer which von Roeder and I killed, together with the fish and oysters caught by four Mexican prisoners in our service, were our chief means of subsistence. We had neither bread, nor coffee, nor sugar, and the water was brackish. Finally, under these distressing circumstances, we became despondent and disheartened; so, late in October, 1836, we boarded our boat, taking along everything we had, including our Mexican prisoners, who acted as oarsmen, and once more made for the mainland, landing at a place called Liverpool, a small village at the head of Chocolate Bayou. The house on Galveston Island was abandoned, there being no one to whom we could sell. There were no other families at that time residing on the island. There were about 400 Mexican prisoners held there in a fort on the eastern shore."

The Klebergs returned to Austin County, where they had made their first settlement, and remained there until 1847, when they removed to De Witt County. Robert Kleberg occupied several positions of public trust and distinction in the Republic, as well as in the later State of Texas. In recognition of his services and ability, President Sam Houston appointed him as early as 1837 one of the associate commissioners of the General Land Office. In 1841 he was commissioned by President Lamar Justice of the Peace, which was then a far more important office than now, as there were few lawyers and few law books at that time, and important and perplexing suits to be decided by these courts. In 1846 he was elected Chief Justice of Austin County, and in 1848 he became one of the commissioners of De Witt County. In 1853 and 1854 he was twice elected Chief Justice of De Witt County. When the war broke out in 1861 he raised a company of volunteers, but on account of his advanced age was not received in active service, but finally appointed as collector of war taxes, which position he occupied during the whole war.

In De Witt County the first school house, a simple log cabin, was built by Robert Kleberg, with the assistance of

Albrecht von Roeder and some American settlers, on Colita Creek, near the old York and Bell farm, in 1849. Hostile Indians then still made occasional raids on the settlements, and the sturdy pioneers had to be forever watchful for the protection and safety of their families.

Robert Kleberg had the good fortune to outlive this period of romance and adventure and to see Texas develop into a great State in wealth and population under the magic wand of civilization, with the proud feeling that he and his family had been active and important factors of its early growth. After the war Judge Kleberg passed the remaining years of his eventful life in quiet repose and composure at Yorktown, De Witt County, where he died surrounded by his family, on October 23, 1888, in his eighty-sixth year, and was buried with Masonic honors. His widow survived him 19 years, being 90 years at her death, which occurred July 3, 1907.

CHAPTER X.
First German Societies in Texas.

The Germans are pre-eminently a sociable people. They cultivate with reverence the strongest family life and family ties, and are bound together in friendship by innumerable social, benevolent and literary societies and secret orders. In all of these societies the "Gemütlichkeit," a term best translated by "good fellowship," predominates, diffusing good cheer among their members. In every city or town in Germany there exist several singing societies, athletic and gun clubs, social, literary, political and secret organizations, all established for the purpose of promoting good comradeship and rendering assistance to the needy. This commendable trait made itself felt with undiminished force among the Germans in Texas. After the first few strenuous years had passed and the German settlements had been firmly established the German's love for sociability, intellectual entertainment, mutual protection and pleasure asserted itself.

The city of Houston founded in August, 1836, by A. C. and J. K. Allen, had become quite a town in the short space of four years. Situated at the head of navigation of Buffalo bayou, it had direct water communication by small craft with the sea and Galveston Island, where the emigrants were landed. None of them remained on the island, which, up to 1839, was uninhabited. All immigrants had to take passage in smaller ships to Harrisburg or Houston, most of them preferring the latter place, which then (1837-1839) was not only the capital of the young Republic, but was also farther inland than Harrisburg. Quite a number of German immigrants stayed in Houston and materially assisted in increasing its population.

By the year 1840 Houston counted among its inhabi-

German Element in Texas 49

tants more than 75 German families and single men. What, then, was more natural than to organize a "Verein"? Consequently a preliminary meeting was held on Sunday, November 22, 1840, in the German boarding house of Franke & Lemsky, corner of Prairie Avenue and Travis Street, at which great enthusiasm prevailed. The organization of a German Society was definitely decided upon, and George Fischer, Henry F. Fischer, Charles Gerlach, Conrad Franke and Theodor Miller were appointed a committee on organization and instructed to draft a constitution and by-laws to be presented to the next meeting and to ask all Germans living in Houston to become members of the proposed society.

On Sunday, November 29, this society was definitely launched under the name "Deutscher Verein für Texas" (German Society of Texas). Its main object, as stated in article II of its constitution, was the giving of assistance to the sick and needy, to promote the material and intellectual welfare of the Germans and to assist newcomers with advice and necessary aid and succor.

This was the first German Society in Texas. It began its long career of usefulness with the following 53 members: George Fischer, Theodor Miller, Henry F. Fischer, Charles Gerlach, Conrad Franke, Robert H. Levenhagen, Henry Levenhagen, Jacob Schroeder, Joseph Sandman, Gottlieb Gasche, Martin Rumpff, William Schroeder, I. Hermann, Gustav Erichson, Jacob Buchmann, I. I. Knoll, A. Jung, Emil Simmler, Friedr. Otto, Ch. Rienitz, Charles Baumann, Henry A. Kuykendall, Wendelin Bock, Ulrich Fischer, Karl Fischer, John H. Mueller, Friedr. Schiermann, John Koop, Daniel Super, Joseph Ehlinger, Johann Buhn, Anton Brueggemann, William Ewald, Casper Gerlach, Friedr. Lemsky, Friedr. Barthold, Dr. K. Hermann Jaeger, Abraham Brodbeck, Johann Grunder, Christian A. Kasting, Peter Dickmann, William Weigand, Ant. E. Spellenberg, Peter Bohl, Johan William Schrimpf, Dr. I.

Anton Fischer, Dr. De Witt, A. Schanten, Johann Schweikart.

The first president of the German Society was George Fischer (he spelled his name Fisher) who, at the town election held on July 8, 1839, had been elected Mayor of Houston, with 115 votes cast for him, while his strongest opponent, George W. Lively, received 112 votes, 37 being cast for Moreau Forest and 65 for William Bronaugh. This gave Fischer only a plurality of votes, although this election was the second held for this office within two weeks; in the first election, held on July 1, eight candidates had aspired to become the administrative head of the rising city, but the result had been very undecisive, the votes being scattered among the eight candidates.

The result of the second election was also contested and the "Morning Star" upon this occasion wrote: "The election of mayor of this city, held on Saturday last, which resulted in favor of George Fisher, was contested before the board of aldermen yesterday, on points of law in such cases provided, and set aside; consequently, the chief justice of the county will take such steps as the law requires to order a new election to be held. This, then, will have been the third election holden in this community for the same office within three weeks or upwards before the will of the people can be ratified. We trust that no negligence to ascertain and observe the laws regulating such election shall occasion us the strife and bickerings of another contest after the next one shall have been decided."

The third election took place July 22, George W. Lively receiving 176, George Fisher 127 votes. The first board of officers of the German Society consisted of of the following: George Fisher, president; Harry Levenhagen, first vice president; Theodore Miller, second vice president; Henry F. Fischer (Fisher), secretary, and John Koop, treasurer. The scope of the society remained localized, but as many of the German immigrants to Texas up to the

60s passed through Houston when going into the interior of the State, it was of material assistance to many of the newcomers by giving them the often greatly needed advice and succor. During the war between the States the society was defunct, but was revived in 1866 as the "Houston Deutsche Gesellschaft" and as such existed until the close of the last century.

The desire of a closer union of the Germans in Texas led to the forming of the Teutonic order, which was organized in 1841 by some settlers of Industry and Cat Spring. The fundamental principle of this order was the uniting of all Texas Germans into one society with strong Germanistic tendencies and thus not only preserving the German character and individuality, but making the Germans a strong political factor in Texas.

In an account of the order, published by Fritz Ernst of Industry, he says: "It remains for the Germans in Texas either to become entirely changed, so as to be called Americans, or to make an attempt in a social way among the Germans living here, to form a New Germany. The former, appears to us, as certainly to all good and true Germans, as entirely impossible and must remain committed to our posterity, while the latter can only be possible and practicable, if all our countrymen be united collectively through a common bond. Concord of thought and action, that disappear but too easily in a foreign land, must be re-established among them and the conscientiousness of their German worth be incited. Since the population of Texas consists of immigrants from different countries who must all consider themselves here as foreigners, it appears that this plan can be carried out more easily in Texas than in North American free States, where a generation born there is the leading race."

Gustav Koerner in his book, "The German Element in North America from 1818-1848," stated the purpose of the order as "the preservation of German natural individuality, the furtherance of German immigration and the facilitation of correspondence between Texas and Germany."—(Koerner, page 359.)

The order was made up of several degrees. Admission to the second and third degrees was conditioned on talent, ability and education. The less educated Germans were almost barred from passing beyond the first degree. The order existed only a few years. The foremost causes of the failure were the evident class distinction between the different degrees and the difficulty of communication between settlements hundreds of miles apart.

Although the Teutonic Order was a failure, it clearly demonstrated the tendency of the German immigrants of the first half of the last century to try the establishment of a New Germany on this side of the Atlantic. Hecke, in his book, had advised the purchase of Texas by Prussia in 1821. Duden and the "Giessener Auswanderungs-Gesellschaft" in 1832, strongly advocated the establishment of one or more German States in the Mississippi Valley or Texas, and the founders of the Teutonic Order were cherishing similar hopes in 1841. The rapid increase in the American population in Texas and the joining of the Republic to the United States in 1845 put an effective stop to these aspirations.

CHAPTER XI.
The Germans in the Republic of Texas.

Texas was an independent Republic from 1836 to 1845. During these nine years it was forever struggling hard for its existence. By far the greater part of its extensive domain was still a wilderness in undisputed possession of the Indians, while, in the settled portion of the great State, many European nationalities, Americans from the United States, Mexicans and negroes, the latter as slaves, were represented. It is impossible to give a correct number of the inhabitants of Texas at that time, as no reliable census figures exist. The statements of travelers in reference to the population of Texas are based only on their personal observations and differ considerably. But we can assume as nearly correct that Texas had about 52,000 white inhabitants in 1836 and 150,000, including the slaves, in 1845, when it was annexed to the United States. On March 2, 1837, the United States had acknowledged the independence of Texas and in 1840 France and Belgium recognized Texas as a sovereign State, but Mexico repudiated the agreement between Santa Anna and President Burnet, by which Texas was declared independent of Mexico, and held Texas as being a province in revolt, and at different times sent military parties into the country. According to the best information obtainable, there were 10,000 Germans in Texas in 1840 and about 20,000 in 1845. According to statistics from 1832 to 1846, 100,000 Germans immigrated from Bremen to America, while many also sailed on ships from Hamburg. During the six years from 1840 to 1846 there arrived at Galveston from Bremen alone 7161 German immigrants, among them many men of culture and refinement who had received a college or university education. They were all induced to seek these shores through love of liberty and partly through the glowing accounts of travelers who had traversed Texas and in their reports did not hesitate to pronounce it the finest country on earth, suitable in every way for colonization by Europeans.

The government of Texas was confronted from the beginning with the constant low ebb of public funds and the difficulty of raising the State's revenues. Several efforts of securing public loans from the United States and England had either failed or proved insufficient, as Texas could pledge as security nothing but millions of acres of land that were of but little actual value at that time, as there was nobody to cultivate them. The import trade of Texas was insignificant and the receipts from import duties were hardly sufficient to pay for the expenses of collection. The public debt constantly increased and the authorities were in a quandary. The only possibility to raise sufficient revenues and put the administration on a self-sustaining basis, seemed to be in the rapid colonization of the vast and fertile lands belonging to the State. It may be added here parenthetically that the inherent rights of the Indians to certain territory were as ruthlessly disregarded by Texas, as anywhere in the United States. The Red men simply had no right whatever to their lands and hunting grounds, when the white man wanted them.

In harmony with the colonization plan of the administration the Texas Congress of 1837 passed a colonization law, similar to the Mexican law of 1824. Each immigrating family was to receive 320 acres of tillable land, each single man 160 acres; large grants were to be made to promoters under the condition of bringing a certain number of settlers to Texas in a specified time. If this condition was complied with to the satisfaction of the General Land Office, the State would give the promoter and the colonists full and undisputed title to the land granted. This liberal land policy proved successful, increasing the population of the Republic from 52,000 in 1836 to 150,000 in

1845, with more than 20,000 Germans included in this number. The actual number of inhabitants of German blood was far greater than 20,000, for this number does not include the children of the immigrants born in Texas, who were considered Texans, and in the later census figures of the United States, were recognized as native born Americans.

In making of land grants the Government did not always act fairly and can not be spared the just criticism of partiality. The more valuable and better protected lands in East Texas were generally reserved for settlers from the United States, while the immigrants from Europe, in the main Germans and several thousand Frenchmen, were given lands in West and South Texas, to act as a bulwark against Indian and Mexican attacks.

The early German immigrants to Texas were mostly agriculturists, with an occasional mixture of mechanics and operatives, but, as Francis J. Grund, in his book, "The Americans," published in 1837, says: "The late unfortunate struggle for liberty in Germany has, within the last five or six years caused the expatriation of a more intelligent class. Settlements have been made in America by a body of Germans whose education fitted them rather for the drawing room and the closet than for the hardships of cultivating the soil; yet they have cheerfully embraced their new vocation."

Although Grund refers only to some German settlements in Illinois and the upper Mississippi Valley, his words apply with the same force to Texas, and it was principally through the directing power of these educated men that the Germans exerted quite an influence in the days of the Republic of Texas.

In 1843 the Texas Congress ordered the laws of Texas to be published in German, and when the Germans began an active campaign for the founding of a German University in Texas, the administration looked favorably on the project, which, of course, seems to have been somewhat utopian. On January 27, 1844, the Texas Congress granted a franchise to the "'Herrmann University," which was to be the "alma mater" of philosophy, medicine, theology and jurisprudence. The professors of these four faculties must be competent to lecture in both the English and German languages, while the professors of theology should not belong to a special religious denomination nor teach doctrines of any sect. Section 7 of the act authorizing the university stated the following, viz: "Section 7. Be it further enacted that no person shall be eligible to a professorship in said university who does not understand both the German and English languages, unless by a unanimous vote of the trustees such qualifications shall be disregarded." This shows plainly the influence and prominence accorded to the German element in Texas at this early period.

The location of the prospective university should be somewhere between the Mill and Cummings Creeks in the present Austin, Colorado or Washington Counties. To the board of regents of the university the authority was granted to levy an excise on spirituous liquors within a radius of 50 miles from the university and a large land grant was issued for its benefit. The management was to consist of one president and 12 trustees. As incorporators of the institution are named: L. C. Ervendberg, F. Ernst, H. Schmidt, H. Amthor, J. G. Lieper, G. Stoehr, F. W. Huesmann and E. Franke.

So far everything seemed propitious for the undertaking, but when the trustees tried to sell the "university shares" they met with insurmountable obstacles. The shares at the par value of $50 could only be sold for land in exchange; nobody paid in cash, money being too scarce. But it was ready cash that the trustees needed, and not land, of which the university had plenty. The attempt to raise the necessary funds proved a failure, and in January, 1846, the franchise was annulled, but was renewed on April 11, 1846.

This time the incorporators were: H. Amthor, E. Franke, H. Draub, H. Ernst, Jacob Rien, E. Miller, E. H. Yordt, Dr. E. Becker, William Trieb, Charles Yordt, Hermann Frels and Ed Ruhmann.

To make the shares more attractive, the subscription price was reduced from $50 to $15. The trustees succeeded in obtaining enough money to build a large, two-story stone building in Frelsburg, but that was all. This building was later used for the public school of Frelsburg, and thus fulfilled its mission in some way, even if it did not bear the proud name of "university."

The plan of establishing a higher institution of learning in Texas in 1845 was premature and not feasible. The Lone Star State had then but a few years ago emerged from the darkness of primitive existence and the magic wand of civilization had but lightly touched it. Even if the trustees had succeeded in procuring sufficient funds for the equipment of the university, there would have been a remarkable scarcity of students. There were no schools in Texas that could prepare pupils for college or universities.

CHAPTER XII.
The Society of German Noblemen.
(Mainzer Aldesverein.)

The German literature about Texas was constantly growing. In a preceding chapter the publications of Hecke, Duden, Arends and Bromme were mentioned, all published between 1821 and 1833. To these were now added the books of F. Hoehne, "Reise Ueber Bremen Nach Nord Amerika und Texas" ("Voyage Over Bremen to North America and Texas, From 1838-1841"), "Das Kajuetenbuch" ("The Cabinbook"), by Charles Sealsfield (Carl Postl), published in Zurich, 1841; Hermann Ehrenberg's "Der Freiheitskampf in Texas" ("The War for Texas' Independence"), Leipzig, 1844; G. A. Scherpf's "Origin and Present Condition of the New State of Texas," published in Augsburg, 1841, and numerous other works of travel. Texas was better advertised and discussed more in German, than any other State of North America. All these books were eagerly read, and as the political, industrial and social conditions in Germany had not improved since 1830, "the mania for emigration," as it was called, increased, and many people were preparing to leave different parts of Germany.

In the novel, "Nathan, the Squatter," published in 1837, Sealsfield dwelt with much emphasis on the picturesque life of the pioneer and the idyllic scenes of life in the thinly populated territory of Texas. We quote the following glowing description of a settlement: "On the level summit of the ridge were situated the plantations of the wealthier planters, and a more beautiful or more favorable settlement you could not imagine. On one side lay what are called clearing lands, from which the primitive forest had just been removed; on the other, immense prairies with the tall grass waving about the heads of the browsing cattle, and horses that were pulling and tumbling against each other like rolling stones; the sound of tinkling cowbells came to our ears in the gentle breeze, and in the far blue distance a thick fog was seen glimmering in the sunbeams through every opening of the vast forest. There was something charming and irresistible in the landscape."

"With the wreck of our fortune, as little as it was competent to support us at home, here it was amply sufficient to gratify every wish of the heart—here I could prepare a home for my betrothed, far from the injuries and storms of the world."

"I found the rudiments—the A B C of squatter life—in the clearings, in the woodland and in the live oaks; the spelling book in the rude and artless dwellings, in the rough furniture made by the backwoodsman himself, in the horses and in the corn stubbles. I saw plainly that I had only to do as the squatters had done to accomplish the same ends. He only, who has to solve the difficult problem of getting along in the backwoods, can form an idea of the childish haste with which I pounced on every object. The log house had irresistible charms. I was in an ecstacy at the thought of the time when my beloved family, in their plain and simple robes, would come to meet me at the cabin door, as I returned from the field."

The above may suffice as a fair example of how Texas and the settlers' life were praised in the different publications of that time. The sentimentality expressed was in full accord with the trend of German feeling during the first half of the last century. It was the age of affected sensibility and lyric poetry, and these books could not but leave a deep impression on their numerous readers.

We have now reached the most interesting stage of the German immigration to Texas. On April 20, 1842, 14 German Princes and noblemen met at Biebrich, on the Rhine, in a conference, the result of which was the forming of a provisional association for the purchase of lands in Texas. The following document was signed by those present:

"We, the undersigned, hereby make known that we have today associated ourselves and are constituted as a society for the purpose of purchasing lands in the free State of Texas. Biebrich, April 20, 1842."

This was the beginning of the society for the protection of German emigrants to Texas, which was formed at a general meeting held at Mainz on March 24, 1844. As only princes and representatives of the higher nobility could become members of it, the society became generally known as the "League of the Nobility" (Adelsverein), of which the following 21 noblemen were the original members, viz.:

Duke Adolf of Nassau, Duke Bernhard Erich of Meiningen, Duke August Ernst of Saxe Coburg, Prince Frederic William Ludwig of Prussia, Prince Günther of Schwarzburg-Rudolstadt, Prince Carl zu Leiningen, Prince Hermann von Wied, Prince Ferdinand von Solms-Braunfels, Prince Franz von Collerado-Mansfield, Prince Otto Victor von Schoenberg-Waldenburg, Prince of Solms-Braunfels Rheingrafenstein, Prince Alexander von Solms-Braunfels, Count Christian von Alt-Leiningen-Westernburg, Count Carl von Isenburg-Meerholz, Count Edmund von Hatzfeld, Count Carl William von Inn und Knyphausen-Lutelsberg, Count Armand von Rennessee, Count Carl von Castell and Baron Paul Scirnay.

The Duke of Nassau accepted the protectorate of the society, Prince Leiningen was elected president and Count Castell secretary and general manager. By a ministerial rescript of the Duchy of Nassau the society was incorporated on March 3, 1844. It was capitalized at 200,000 gulden ($80,000), consisting of 40 shares at 5000 gulden ($2000) each. Shortly after the first meeting at Biebrich in 1842, the "Adelsverein," as this galaxy of princes and noblemen will henceforth be called, had dispatched

Counts Victor von Leiningen and Boos-Waldeck to Texas with ample funds and full power to purchase land from the Texas Government. They arrived in Galveston in the beginning of September, and in Houston on September 13, from which place both went to San Felipe de Austin and Industry. From there Count Leiningen went to Austin to confer with President Sam Houston in reference to land grants and special concessions he expected to receive for the colonization project of the Adelsverein. It is very probable that he would have succeeded if he had not made the mistake of asking too much. One of his demands was that the colonists should be exempt from taxation for a number of years. This, of course, could not be granted, as the liberal land policy of Texas had for its main object the quick increase of the State's revenues, of which the Administration was sorely in need. If Count Leiningen had been properly advised, or if he had shown some business ability and consideration for existing conditions, there can be but little doubt that he would have succeeded in obtaining the desired land grant from President Houston and thus a great deal of expense and trouble would have been saved the Adelsverein. But fate had decreed differently. After his negotiations at Austin had terminated without any results, Leiningen returned to Germany in 1843, and reported favorably for a wholesale colonization in Texas. A wholesale colonization without a foot of ground belonging to the Verein!

Count Boos-Waldeck in the meantime, following the advice of Mr. Ernst, the founder of Industry, had bought in Fayette County a fine plantation of 4428 acres for 54,-000 gulden ($22,000), which he christened "Nassau," and which was destined to play an important part in the history of the Adelsverein. A large dwelling house, stables, barn and outhouses were on the farm, which was cultivated by negroes, who also became the property of the Adelsverein.

Boos-Waldeck returned to Germany in 1844 and in his

report advised against a colonization on an extensive scale because the expenses of such an undertaking would be too high. Unfortunately his warning voice was disregarded and the vague proposition of Count Leiningen adopted. The unpardonable carelessness, not to say imbecility, of the managers of the Adelsverein, in carrying out their plan will be demonstrated in succeeding chapters.

West of San Antonio a Frenchman by the name of Henry Castro had received a land grant and established there a colony of Alsatians and Belgians. North of it another Frenchman, Bourgeois (d'Orvanne) had received another grant that was forfeited in 1843 for noncompliance with its conditions. North of this grant, in the present counties of Kendall and Gillespie, Count Leiningen was offered a grant, but refused to accept it on the ground that it was too far west and too far from the sea. While this objection was well founded, still he should have either accepted the offer, as he was told that he could receive no other grant, or his advice to the Adelsverein should have been against a wholesale colonization.

CHAPTER XIII.
The Adelsverein Buys a Land Grant Which Proves Worthless.

When the recommendations of Count Waldeck were rejected by the officers of the Adelsverein, he withdrew as a member of the society. This was rather unfortunate for the "Verein," as it seems that he was the only member with a fair understanding of the conditions in Texas and the proper requirements for a successful colonization. The affairs of the Adelsverein from now on were exclusively in the hands of its general manager, Count Castell. It is a mooted question whether his boundless enthusiasm for the project carried him beyond the limits of prudence and caution, or whether he possessed any business ability at all, acting simply under orders of his superiors. Be that as it may, his business transactions proved ruinous for the Adelsverein. During the summer of 1843 there arrived in Germany a Frenchman, named Bourgeois, who had come directly from Texas and who had a land —or colonization—grant from the Republic west of San San Antonio. He had ennobled himself by adding the suffix d'Orvanne to his name. Presenting himself to Count Castell as the Chevalier Bourgeois d'Orvanne, he quickly enthralled Castell by his eloquence and the glowing description of his grant, which, as he stated, had unlimited possibilities for colonization. This concession he offered to sell to the Adelsverein. When he did that the time limit for colonization under his grant had almost expired. The grant to Bourgeois was dated July 3, 1842, and under its conditions he had to settle 400 families on the land during the 18 months following. The time, therefore, expired on December 3, 1843, but he declared it would be an easy matter to receive an extension of the time limit on application, from President Sam Houston, who was his personal friend. After many conferences deferred through the customary procrastination in official matters, Bourgeois' land concession was finally bought by the Adelsverein on April 7, 1844, after it had virtually expired four months previously and contrary to the advice of Count Waldeck.

Then the Adelsverein issued the following program, which was published in many newspapers of Germany: "An association has been formed having for its aim to guide as much as possible immigration into one favorable direction, to support the immigrants during their long journey, and to secure for them new homes across the sea.

"The association does not publish this announcement with a view to procure funds for their undertaking—the necessary capital having already been signed—but, conscious of a righteous cause, the association feels in duty bound to itself and the public, to lay before the latter the motives that have called this association into existence, the ways and means by which they hope to effect their object and the principles by which they are guided.

"The association neither means to further, nor excuse the tendency for emigration. That the exigency exists can neither be denied nor checked. Many causes are at work to bring this condition about. Manual labor being suppressed by machinery; the great, almost periodic, crises that overwhelm commerce; the increasing poverty as a result of over population and lack of employment, and finally perhaps the much lauded richness of the soil in the new world; but, above all, an expectation, sometimes realized, but just as often deceived, of a happier life across the ocean.

"Under such circumstances the emigrants would certainly better their lot, if, by keeping together in a well organized body, they could find proper guidance and protection in the foreign land. Thus the necessity for the association and its aims are at once explained. It wishes to regulate and guide emigration for the purpose of the Germans finding a German home in America, and that by maintaining an unbroken connection between themselves and the Fatherland, an industrial and commercial intercourse may arise that must be materially and intellectually beneficial to both. In this manner the association wishes to contriblute its share to Germany's glory and honor, in order to afford to the German poor in future a field of fruitful labor, to open new markets to German industry and to give to German sea trade a wider expansion.

"After long and careful deliberation the Verein has reached the conclusion that Texas is pre-eminently the country that will suit the German emigrant best. The association has sent experienced men to Texas, who have traveled through that country far and near and have given such information that the Verein could make its selection conscientiously and unhesitatingly.

"The association has acquired in the healthiest part of the country a continuous, uncultivated territory of considerable extent, where it will assist, as much as possible, the settling of those Germans who wish to leave their native country, and to that end will use those means best adapted to existing conditions.

"Before departure a tract of good land will be guaranteed in writing to each emigrant, which he receives as a present from the association without any compensation whatsoever."

The program then contains certain conditions under which the emigrants are to be carried across the sea, the rules and regulations of the prospective colony and the statement that each single man must deposit with the association 300 gulden ($120) and each head of an average family 600 gulden ($240). It concludes with the following admonitions:

."The new fatherland across the ocean can only thrive, when the Germans there continue to be as they were at home; thrifty, painstaking and loyal to sound morals and the laws. Although the association has no doubts in this regard, it will only admit to emigration 150 families during this year, and only after these emigrants have established a well secured settlement, will the Verein assist in further emigration."

The executive committee:

(Sig.) Prince zu Leiningen,
Count Isenburg-Merholz,
for the absent Count Castell.

Mainz, April 9, 1844.

(For full text of the program in German see Appendix C.)

After the Adelsverein had thus made its intentions known to the German people, Prince Carl Solms-Braunfels was appointed commissioner general for the colony and Bourgeois d'Orvanne as his assistant with the title of colonial director. Both departed for Texas in May to make the necessary arrangements for the expected first shipload of emigrants. Bourgeois tried to obtain an extension of his forfeited land concession from President Sam Houston, but failing in this, Prince Solms was constrained to write in a private letter to Count Castell "that they were in the embarrassing position of having emigrants coming with no lands to grant them." If the prince had added, that land in West Texas could then be bought at from 5 to 15 cents per acre, the prospects of the enterprise might have been different, from what they became through another hasty and senseless purchase of a second land grant, of which we shall speak in the next chapter. Bourgeois d'Orvanne had been informed on August 24, 1844, that he was no longer a member of the association and that his services as colonial director were no longer required, while

Prince Solms with his suite was traveling over Texas in search of suitable lands for the expected colonists. In his reports to the directorate of the Adelsverein, Prince Solms had declared the large plantation, Nassau, bought by Count Boos-Waldeck in Fayette County, to be undesirable for the colonization projects of the Verein, because it was too close to other settlements, and, therefore, not adapted for a German colony, that should be established where the German colonist would be unmolested from interference by other settlers, in order to preserve their National customs and religion. This decision of the prince was very unfortunate, as the plantation would have furnished an admirable stopping place for the immigrants on their long road to the land grant in West Texas that the Adelsverein bought after the Bourgeois grant had been forfeited. The latter's concession had not been favored by Prince Solms either, "because it was too far from the coast in order to carry on trade with Mexico," as he wrote to the Verein. Despite this Count Castell negotiated the purchase of a land grant still 100 miles further northwest, thus dooming the colonization enterprise of the Adelsverein to failure, before it had actually begun.

CHAPTER XIV.
Purchase of a Second Land Grant by the Adelsverein.

In the spring of 1844 there arrived in Bremen a German Texan by the name of Henry Francis Fisher (Heinrich Franz Fischer), commissioned as consul for Texas. Fisher came from Houston, where he was engaged in the general land business, being also a notary public and secretary of the German Society for Texas. He and a certain Burchard Miller (Burkart Mueller), also of Houston, had obtained an immense land concession in West Texas from President Sam Houston on September 1, 1843. The grant provided, among other conditions, that Fisher and Miller should settle on that land 600 families from Europe in 18 months, with a later total of 6000 families. The time limit expired on March 1, 1945, and all the lands of the grant remained property of the State until the conditions were fulfilled. If Fisher and Miller should bring the required number of immigrants from Europe in the specified time, then the State would give proper title to these immigrants after they had lived on the claim for three successive years, built a house and fenced in at least 15 acres. Each family would receive title to 640 acres (one section), each single man 320 acres. But the contractors had permission to make contract with each emigrant for transfer of not more than half of this land to the contractor.

When Fisher arrived in Germany nearly one year of the time limit of his contract had already elapsed. Later the Texas Legislature, on January 20, 1845, granted an extension of time until March 1, 1846, but when Fisher began negotiations in Germany for colonizing the land of his grant there were but 10 months left for sending the emigrants to Texas. Fisher had obtained from Count Boos-Waldeck, whom he had told that he intended to visit Germany, a letter of introduction to Count Castell on November 10, 1843, while Waldeck was in Galveston. This letter he sent to Count Castell from Bremen on March 12, 1844, stating that he would come to Mainz at the earliest possible time to lay before the directorate of the Adelsverein his colonization plan. Count Castell acknowledged receipt of this communication on May 18, stating that he would be pleased to confer with Consul Fisher on this project, adding that he had already written several times to Count Boos-Waldeck to open negotiations with Mr. Fisher, but that he had refused to do so, because he believed a colonization on the Fisher and Miller grant an impossibility. Count Waldeck's advice was again disregarded, and on June 24, 1844, the Adelsverein bought the land contract of Fisher and Miller, paying $9000 in three deferred payments and assuming to carry out all the conditions demanded by the State of Texas.

The original Fisher and Miller land grant dated from June 7, 1842, but was renewed as "Fisher and Miller's second contract" on September 1, 1843, and, as stated above, again extended by the Texas Legislature on January 29, 1845, to March 1, 1846. The lands of this concession lay on the southern banks of the Colorado River, between the Llano and San Saba Rivers, the nearest points to existing settlements being about 100 miles west of Austin, 150 miles from San Antonio and almost 300 miles from the sea coast. The whole tract contained, according to an official statement of the Adelsverein (Handbook for Emigrants, Bremen, 1846, page 80), 3,878,000 acres. That almost half of this territory was unsuited for agricultural purposes, being traversed by the San Saba mountain ridge, was not mentioned, probably because nobody then knew anything definite about the topography of the San Saba country. Fisher had never seen the land, yet he declared unhesitatingly that it was all fine farming land and that the Adelsverein could easily settle there 6000 families with the expense of $80,000. It seems that Count Castell was hypnotized by the great extent of the territory, the same being about ten times the size of the dukedom of Nassau, for he implicitly believed in all that Fisher said, whose sole interest in the matter was the quick disposal of his claim, and, without waiting for any information about the land from Prince Solms, who, as we know, was in Texas, he entered into a contract with Henry F. Fisher, purchasing unknown lands that no white man had yet visited, lands inhabited by the savage and hostile Comanche Indians, and assuming onerous conditions that the Adelsverein was utterly unable to fulfill. One of the conditions of the State of Texas was that the contractor had to survey the land at his own expense, dividing the same into sections of 620 acres, each alternate section remaining the property of the State, while the State did not promise any assistance against the Indians, who might object to being deprived of their customary hunting grounds.

The surveying of the tract alone later cost the Adelsverein about $80,000, in other words, the full amount for which it was capitalized.

According to the contract (Uebereinkunft) between Count Castell, as representative of the Adelsverein and Henry F. Fisher, representing the proprietors of Fisher and Miller's land grant, signed at Mainz on June 24, 1844, article 3, (section 2), Fisher and Miller were to receive one-third of all the profits made by the Verein through the sale of lands, or from industrial establishments, while they agreed not to sell their interests in the enterprise before 1848 to anybody, even if they were offered more than the Adelsverein was willing to pay.

Previous to any profit sharing the Adelsverein had, of course, to be reimbursed for all expenses made in the interest of the colonization project. In order to protect the interests of both contracting parties, section 3 of article 3, created a colonial committee (Colonialrath) in which the Adelsverein had five and Fisher and Miller three votes. To this colonial committee was granted exclusive executive power in all colonization matters, and Fisher could appoint a substitute in his place. The officers of this colonial committee were to be in Texas and during Fisher's absence Burchard Miller had power of attorney to represent their interests (article 6, paragraph 3). But it seems that Prince Solms did not recognize Miller's authority, for in a letter to Fisher, dated Houston, April 10, 1845, Miller complains bitterly about the treatment he received from the Prince, who had said that the Adelsverein did not know Miller, and that he (Miller) had no business whatever in the colonial committee or the colonization project. He calls the Prince's attitude a "bombastic boast, such as could only be imported from Germany."

On December 14, 1844, the directorate of the Adelsverein had to acknowledge the failure of the purchase of Bourgeois' land contract through the publication of the following notice: "The grant of Bourgeois d'Orvanne has been declared forfeited by the Congress of Texas, but the company has made another contract with H. Fisher, by which the more northerly situated, extraordinarily fertile and healthy lands on the right banks of the Colorado River have been acquired (!) and come into possession of the Adelsverein.   The Directorate."

This statement is either intentionally misleading, or Count Castell was unable to properly interpret the meaning of the contract entered into between the Adelsverein and Fisher and Miller. The latter had no land to sell and the former had only acquired the privilege to settle a certain number of emigrants on a certain tract of land that remained in possession of the Republic of Texas until certain conditions were fulfilled, when the State would execute deeds to the colonists. For each 100 families who settled on the grant the contractors would receive 10 sections of land of 640 acres each, and for each 100 single men, 10 half sections of 320 acres each. This was the gist of the contract, yet it seems that the Adelsverein, as many writers (Kapp, Siemering, von Rosenberg, von Meusebach) contend, was under the impression that it owned several million acres in Texas, which it could either give or sell to the prospective colonists, or where large landed estates for such members of the German nobility could be established, who were barred from inheriting land in Germany by the law of progeniture.

CHAPTER XV.
Colonization Under the Auspices of the Adelsverein.

After the purchase of Fisher and Miller's land grant the Adelsverein was ready to proceed with its colonization project, and preparations were made to send to Texas the first party of emigrants. The association entered into a mutual agreement with each emigrant, in which the Verein in consideration of the payment of 300 or 600 gulden ($120 or $240) not only promised to bring the emigrants to Texas, but also to furnish free transportation from the place of landing to the colony in wagons and tents of the society, and the furnishing of a rude dwelling, to be built on their lands in the colony. This the Adelsverein expected to accomplish for half of the amount of money deposited by each emigrant. The other half was credited to the emigrants who could draw on it for farming implements or extra rations from the company's stores until they had made their first crops. The officials of the Adelsverein had calculated that the cost of transportation from Galveston to Port Lavaca and from there to the point of destination (about 300 miles) would be $4 per head, and that a log house could be furnished for $24, while in fact the transportation of each emigrant cost the Adelsverein about $20 and a house could not be built for less than $100. Neither Count Castell nor any other official of the association had the slightest idea of the conditions, prices or cost of living in Texas, and neither Bourgeois nor Fisher found it to their interest to enlighten the German officials on these important points. Bourgeois d'Orvanne and Henry F. Fisher were the evil spirits of the Adelsverein and it was primarily their scheming and misrepresentations that caused the early collapse of the enterprise. But this can in no wise excuse the stupendous incompetency and childish credulity of Count Castell and other officials of the Verein, whose actions were an unbroken chain of gigantic blunders.

The association agreed furthermore to give to each head of a family a provisional title for 320 acres of land and to each single man for 160 acres, which title would be perfected after three years of continuous living on the land by the Government of Texas, but the colonist had to reimburse the Verein for the cost of survey and settle all other indebtedness to the association before he could receive a clear title. During the first three years the colonists were also subject to regulations established by the Adelsverein, as well as to the laws of Texas. Thus everything seemed to be properly arranged, and in September, 1844, the first party of emigrants assembled in Bremen to sail to the promised land.

Prince Solms-Braunfels, the commissioner general, with the German members of the colonial committee, and Bourgeois d'Orvanne had arrived at Galveston on July 1, 1844. Prince Solms' first sad experience was the information that Bourgeois' land grant had been forfeited and would neither be extended nor renewed. Thus he was temporarily the executive head of a colonization company without an acre of land, except the plantation Nassau. The situation was hardly improved when he was informed of the purchase of the Fisher and Miller grant and when he found that the land was almost 300 miles inland, in a wilderness, inhabited by dangerous tribes of hostile savages and far removed from access to the actual necessities of life.

On November 23, 1844, the brig Johann Dethard from Bremen, arrived at Galveston with the first emigrants for the new colony, followed in December by the Ferdinand and Herschel, bringing in all 200 families of about 700 people, with their belongings, all anxious to be transported as quickly as possible to their future homes. This, under the circumstances stated above, was impossible, and

Prince Solms, who received the immigrants at Galveston, was at first nonplused. The first thing to do was to bring the immigrants to the mainland and there await further developments. The immigrants were told that the lands of the Verein could not be reached at the present time for various reasons, but they would be well taken care of by the Adelsverein until they could be installed on their promised lands.

Among the passengers of the first emigrant ship of the Adelsverein were quite a number of well-educated men, who were willing for the sake of personal freedom to change their life of comparative ease and comfort in a civilized country to the life of toil and hardship of a pioneer in an uncivilized land, and endure all privations and inconveniences of the frontiersmen in uninhabited regions. Mention should be made of Fritz Goldbeck, who came to Texas with his parents in the ship Johann Dethart in 1844. He was then only fourteen years old and with his family experienced all the troubles of these early days. He was the first German—Texas poet, ,having written a great number of poems, which, in a simple and unpretending language, are descriptive of the settlers' life on the prairies of Texas, and bring to memory many interesting facts and occurrences of the primitive days of the Lone Star State. In 1865 he was appointed Mayor of New Braunfels by Governor Davis, and later re-elected. The last years of his life, after having traveled extensively in Mexico and California, Mr. Goldbeck passed in San Antonio, where he died in 1900, at the age of 70 years. It may be interesting to note that of the descendants of the families of Goldbeck and Mueller, his wife's family, who came to Texas in 1844 and 1848, seventeen members strong, now still four members are living in San Antonio and Fredericksburg, these being Mrs. F. Goldbeck and three sisters. (Appendix D contains a few of the poems of Fritz Goldbeck in German, which are selected from his book, "Seit fünfzig Jahren" (For fifty years), published in 1895 at San Antonio.)

All immigrants were first transported by small craft to Matagorda Bay, about 100 miles southwest of Galveston, and landed at Indianport, later Indianola, or Carlshafen, as Prince Solms christened the place. There the colonists celebrated their first Christmas in the new world, and although the prince tried to make it as comfortable and pleasant for them as possible, many were the tears shed at the thoughts of their far away homes and the uncertain prospects of the near future. In tents and hastily constructed wooden sheds the immigrants remained at Carlshafen for over two months before the slow and tedious march into the interior began, while Prince Solms was hunting for a proper place to establish the first relay station for his proteges. By the aid of Dr. Ferdinand Lindheimer, a well known botanists, who had been in Texas since 1836, he was fortunate to find such a place at "Las Fontanas" on the Comal and Guadaloupe Rivers. He bought 1300 acres of land for $800, on March 14, 1845, and seven days later, on March 21, the wearied colonists struck camp there, after a long and tiresome march of 150 miles. The company's engineers at once platted part of the land for a city and thus the first German settlement in West Texas was born and christened New Braunfels, after the family castle of Prince Solms on the Lahn River. The colonists received each a town lot free of charge and the families each 10 acres of adjoining land, which gifts in no way invalidated their previous claims on 160, or 320 acres of the land grant. Then the colonists quickly built their log houses in the new town, while on an elevation a larger house for the prince and the officers of the company was built, to which Prince Solms gave the somewhat euphemistic name of "Sophienburg."

During all this time the Adelsverein, according to its contract with the emigrants, had to provide them with means of subsistence and this had to be continued in New Braunfels until the colonists could harvest and dispose of their first crop. This constant drain on the association's treasury increased in proportion with the arrival of more immigrants during 1845, and, being far in excess of the calculations based on Henry F. Fisher's information, was one of the chief reasons of the early collapse of the Adelsverein.

Prince Carl zu Solms-Braunfels was a true cavalier of the old regime. A gentleman by birth and breeding, he was of a genial, prepossessing disposition, kind and obliging, stately in appearance and demeanor, with every advantage for court life and the drawing room. Transferred to the prairies of Texas and the life of the frontiersman, he could not but fail with even the best of intentions. His appointment as executive head of the German immigration in Texas was another stupendous blunder of the Adelsverein. Prince Solms was just as deficient in business ability as Count Castell, the general manager in Germany, and their combined management or rather mismanagement of affairs of the Adelsverein could only end in disaster. After the founding of New Braunfels and the building of the Sophienburg, Prince Solms unexpectedly returned to Germany, leaving to his successor the affairs in a condition bordering on chaos. He had stayed there but little over one month and departed before his successor had arrived.

He never returned to Texas, but when the citizens of New Braunfels, at the twenty-fifth anniversary of their city, cabled the prince their greetings he acknowledged the courtesy with the following cabled message:

To the Citizens of New Braunfels:

My sincerest thanks for your kind remembrance at the jubilee of the city of New Braunfels. It surprised me as much as I was delighted over it.

Glory and happiness to those who have manfully established their homes in the new country.

May God give continued blessing and prosperity to my beloved fellow countrymen at New Braunfels. Do not forget me, as I am thinking of you often in faithful affection.

Carl Prince zu Solms,

K. K. (Imperial Royal) Field Marshal Lieutenant.
Wiesbaden, May 6, 1870.

CHAPTER XVI.
Further German Immigration Under the Adelsverein in 1845.

Prince Solms was in such haste to leave New Braunfels that he did not await the arrival of his successor, Baron Otfried, Hans von Meusebach, who had been appointed commissioner general on February 24, 1845. When von Meusebach arrived, he soon saw that the finances of the association were in a hopeless condition. The company's treasurer, being ordered to make out a complete statement of all assets, credits and obligations of the Adelsverein in Texas, could not comply with the order. He explained to Meusebach that the prince, the treasurer, the doctor, the engineer and other officials had issued orders, due bills, drafts and notes promiscuously, and that no proper account of them had been kept in the company's books. Meusebach, a man of great energy, at once decided to follow Prince Solms to Galveston, and obtain from him the desired information as to the financial standing of the Verein in Texas. He met the prince in Galveston and it seems best to let von Meusebach speak for himself about their meeting. In "Answers to Interrogatories," pages 12-13, he says:

"I found Prince Solms there with an attachment against him, taken out by some uneasy creditor of the company. I lifted the attachment by paying the claim out of my credit of $10,000 under the condition that he would urge the directorate in Europe to send immediately, and, without waiting for a report, a credit twice as much as I had along, because the items of indebtedness picked up by me on the road from Carlshafen to New Braunfels and from there to Galveston showed the association being in debt to that amount. I told him that the welfare of the immigrants depended for the present on the means of the company that had promised to support them in provisions until they could raise a crop and to furnish them with everything necessary to make a crop either for pay, or on credit.

"I have no doubt that the prince did notify the directory in Europe according to promise. But that committee probably had at that time no more available funds on hand. Having failed to get from the prince in Galveston any reliable information in regard to the financial operations of the company and its debts and having been referred again to the treasurer at New Braunfels, who had declared that he could not make a full statement, I had to go to work at it myself. I restored order in the financial department and by close management inspired the creditors with confidence and would have kept both order and confidence, but for some new stupendous blunder on the part of the directory in Europe in the shipment of the emigrants in the fall of 1845. In August, 1845, I had sent a complete statement of all amounts, credits and debits of the company in Texas showing that a debt of $19,460.02 was left by my predecessor in office, besides using up my own credit of $10,000 for provisions for the immigrants at New Braunfels. By the first of November this debt had increased to $24,000 and I requested the directorate in Europe to send immediately this amount as a separate fund irrespective of the amounts necessary for the reception of the new immigrants to be shipped in the fall of 1845, and for further operations."

If the Adelsverein had been true to its public declarations and its pledge it would have remitted the amount asked for, but von Meusebach's urgent request was never complied with. In fact, the association was practically bankrupt there and then and it was only due to the great activity of Meusebach and his astonishing resourcefulness that the sinking ship was kept afloat for some time longer.

Von Meusebach knew that he had to expect several thousand new immigrants by November of that year and that it was absolutely necessary to establish another station nearer the land grant, if the colonists should ever reach it. Therefore, with a small exploring party, he left New Braunfels in the latter part of August, advancing in a northwesterly direction towards the Llano River, being the first white man penetrating into that country. About 75 miles from New Braunfels he found the desired location near the banks of the Pedernales River, it being about two-thirds of the distance to the nearest boundary line of the grant. There he bought 10,000 acres of arable land, well watered and timbered, on credit, equipped and sent out a surveying party of 26 men, led by Lieutenant Bene, in December and had a wagon road established from New Braunfels to the new settlement. The whole tract was laid out in 10-acre lots and distributed among immigrants of 1845 and 1846 as preliminary homesteads. This was the beginning of Fredericksburg, today the county seat of Gillespie County and one of the most flourishing German settlements in Texas.

When von Meusebach had left Europe for Texas at the end of February, 1845, he had been informed that the Adelsverein intended to send a considerable number of emigrants to Texas in the fall. And they came. When he returned from his exploring expedition to New Braunfels at the end of October, he found letters awaiting him with the information that 4000 emigrants were on their way to Texas and that a credit to the amount of $24,000 had been opened for him with a banker of New Orleans, in other words a credit of $6 for each emigrant. For this pittance the emigrants had to be transported from Galveston to the mainland, thence to New Braunfels (later to Fredericksburg) and given provisions until they had made their first crop. That the association's debt in Texas at that time was already more than the new credit opened for Meusebach, the directors in Mainz seemed to have either forgotten, or held it beneath their dignity to notice, or were under the impression that, having paid their debt of $24,000 with the amount sent to New Orleans, Meusebach would enjoy an unlimited credit.

Through private letters of Prince Solms, through his personal report, which he undoubtedly made after his return to Germany, and through the detailed reports of von Meusebach, coupled with his urgent request for further funds, the Adelsverein must have been fully acquainted with the Verein's condition in Texas, its obligation and the cost of transportation and support of the immigrants. At the ridiculously low estimate of 10 cents for daily rations to each person, this alone would have amounted to $45,000 for 5000 people in three months, while the transportation from Galveston to New Braunfels would increase the expenses to about $40,000 more. Still it seems that Count Castell was laboring under the happy illusion that $24,000 would last indefinitely, while, in fact, the following amounts were necessary in Texas by the fall of 1845, viz.:

1. Forty-five thousand dollars for provisions for 5000 persons for three months.

2. Twenty-five thousand dollars for the payment of the floating debt.

3. Thirty-five thousand dollars for transportation of 4000 immigrants to New Braunfels.

4. Fifteen thousand dollars to build about 200 houses in the colony.

Total, $120,000. (Meusebach, "Answers to Interrogatories.")

This would have placed the Verein's affairs in Texas on a sound business basis and the immigrants would have been saved many hardships and great distress. But instead there was only the paltry sum of $24,000 available, barely sufficient to liquidate the floating debt. (Meusebach, "Answers to Interrogatories.")

This sending of 4000 immigrants in the fall and winter of 1845 probably was the most inexcusable of the many blunders of the Adelsverein. Through Prince Solms, who had returned to Germany in August, 1845, Count Castell was made fully aware of the precarious condition of the colonists who had come to Texas in December, 1844, and the impossibility of reaching the grant lands for some time. Despite this undisputable fact, he sent over 4000 more immigrants who had to be housed and supported for an indefinite period.

The proper policy would have been to send the immigrants in small numbers, to buy from ten to 20,000 acres of lands every 30 miles apart and there establish settlements as relay stations, and thus advance gradually from the coast to the proposed colony in the Fisher and Miller grant. This would have insured success, provided, of course, that the financial affairs in Germany were conducted on a sound business basis. As it was, there were only the two settlements, New Braunfels and Fredericksburg, on the entire distance of more than 250 miles from the coast to the grant, New Braunfels being 150 miles from Indianola, and Fredericksburg 75 miles further, with no intermediate resting places.

Robert Penninger's "Festival Edition" for the celebration of the fiftieth anniversary of Fredericksburg (May, 1896), contains a detailed and interesting account of the founding of this German colony in the Western wilderness of Texas, from which we quote the following: "In the middle of December, 1845, Commissioner General von Meusebach sent out from New Braunfels an expedition of 36 men under the command of Lieutenant and Surveyor Bene, with instructions to establish a wagon road from New Braunfels to the north banks of the Pedernales, where he had bought land for a new settlement.

This expedition was well equipped with wagons, provisions, weapons, instruments and tools, and besides Lieutenant Bene, two engineers, Gross and Murcheson, accompanied it. They arrived at their point of destination after a march of three weeks, and at once began the construction of a block house, which was only partly finished, when they were forced to return to New Braunfels for lack of supplies.

On April 24, 1846, the first body of colonists started for the new settlement in 20 heavy ox-carts and some Mexican two-wheeled vehicles, amid the cheers of their countrymen, who remained at New Braunfels. When they approached the Pedernales they were met by a number of Indians from the tribe of the Delawares, who, fortunately, were friendly disposed and the colonists passed the Indian camp unmolested.

Friday, May 8, the weary immigrants reached the place where the surveying party had begun the erection of the first house of the new colony in an opening of the virgin forest of gigantic trees and dense coppice. The new settlement, named Fredericksburg, in honor of Prince Frederick of Prussia, a member of the Adelsverein, was platted by Surveyor Wilke, the fearless pioneers began the construction of their new homes, their number being constantly increased by the arrival of new immigrants, and soon Fredericksburg had 1000 busy and industrious inhabitants. Through gifts and considerate treatment they succeeded in establishing and maintaining friendly relations with the Indians who were quite numerous, and, like New Braunfels, Fredericksburg suffered very little from Indian depredations. It would have been an easy matter for the Indians of the Llano and San Saba territory to destroy Fredericksburg, as well as the settlements of Betina, Castell and Leiningen, that were established in 1847, but all the Indians had great respect for von Meusebach, whom they called "El Sol Colorado," from his flow-ing beard, and the German Indian Agent Emil Krieswitz was very prudent and circumspect in his dealings with the different Indian tribes and secured the friendship of their chiefs for the German pioneers.

CHAPTER XVII.
Arrival of More Than Five Thousand German Immigrants in 1845-46.

With hardly any funds on hand whatever and with thousands of immigrants to be taken care of on their way to Texas, von Meusebach was not in an enviable position. A man with less sense of duty would have resigned at once, while a man with less energy and resourcefulness than Meusebach would have been in a hopeless embarrassment. But fortunately Meusebach was equal to the emergency. He knew that the immigrants trusted the Adelsverein implicitly and now he bent all his energies to take care of the coming flood of immigrants in the best manner possible. He went to Galveston to see after their disembarkation and further transportation, first to Carlshafen (Indianola) and thence to New Braunfels.

From October, 1845, to April, 1846, there arrived at Galveston 5247 immigrants in 36 ships, 24 of which came from Bremen and 12 from Antwerp. They all, after disembarking, had to be brought by small schooners to Lavaca Bay, and, as most of the immigrants had very heavy and often bulky baggage, and provisions for four months had also to be transferred from the vessels to Carlshafen, this was quite a difficult task, but nothing in comparison with the strenuous exertions to be made for the transportation from Indianola to New Braunfels.

Through Meusebach's efforts the immigrants were brought from Galveston to Indianola as speedily as possible and housed in tents and barracks, while he was searching the country for teams to transport the several thousand people to New Braunfels and Fredericksburg. After many unsuccessful efforts he finally made a contract with Torrey Brothers of Houston, in March, 1846, for the transportation of the immigrants from Indianola to New Braunfels, who in the meantime had been subjected to great sufferings and diseases. The winter of 1845-46 in Texas unfortunately was exceedingly severe and wet, rain falling almost continuously for months. Many of the immigrants being badly housed and poorly nourished, contracted fever and several hundred of them died at Indianola during the winter. The suffering was intense and everybody hailed with joy the announcement made in March, that relief could be expected daily and that the march to the colony would soon begin. Shortly after that 100 teams arrived and the first wagon train started for the interior. Then the war between the United States and Mexico broke out (May, 1846), the American commanders utilizing all available horses in Texas; the United States Government paid more for teams than Meusebach could afford, Torrey & Co. repudiated their contract and the immigrants were left to their own resources. Five hundred enlisted with the American army, while the others started on the road, trying to reach New Braunfels the best way they could. This proved disastrous to many, more than 200 perishing on the way from exposure, hunger and exhaustion; the bleached bones of the dead everywhere marked the road of death the unfortunate people had taken, while those who arrived at New Braunfels and later at Fredericksburg carried with them germs of disease that soon developed into a frightful epidemic, in which more than 1000 died.

The conditions at New Braunfels and Fredericksburg soon became exasperating. Most of the colonists were dissatisfied and restless, because they felt that they were imposed upon by the association, and when the deadly disease began to spread and the stipulated daily rations of the "Verein" were no longer distributed regularly, the affairs bordered almost on anarchy. Von Meusebach was threatened with bodily harm and he had to employ all his powers of persuasiveness to quiet the excited men and women, promising them with great eloquence that in the near future everything would be well and that the colonists would soon sit under their own fig trees on their own land in the colonial possessions. Thus he skilfully abated the storm and comparative order was restored, although many of the colonists, believing that the end of their existence was near, indulged in senseless dissipations and wild revelries, refusing to work under any consideration. The outlook was gloomy with every indication that both colonies of the Adelsverein were doomed to speedy extinction. While the scurvy epidemic was at its height, men and women became bereft of reason, all family ties were broken and the wretched people tried to forget their misery by dancing, carousing and drinking. Dr. Koester, the only physician at New Braunfels, was powerless against the attacks of the disease, which only spent its force after one-third of the inhabitants had fallen victims to its deadly grip (Dr. Frederic Kapp says two-thirds, A. Soergel, who was one of the immigrants at New Braunfels, says one-third, while von Meusebach asserts that "the total did not much overrun 800 or 850").

During most of this ill-fated period Meusebach was practically without funds for the support of the colonists. He sent urgent reports to the directory in Germany for the immediate forwarding of money, but his requests were not heeded. Then he went to the farm Nassau and bought from the rich planters on the Brazos provisions of any kind on credit; he tried to raise money in Houston and New Orleans, but failed, the banker of the Adelsverein at the latter place refusing to advance funds for the reason that he had no confidence whatever in an enterprise that was begun and carried on with such a stupendous lack of business ability. Returning to Galveston, Meusebach stated the precarious condition of the finances to the Verein's agent, Klaener, who had to admit that he also was in a predicament to such an extent that he had been forced to hypothecate his store with all its contents. Then Meusebach resorted to the last expediency—publicity. He advised Klaener to send a correct report of the miserable conditions as they actually existed, to some reputed newspaper in Germany, requesting publication of the article. Klaener followed Meusebach's advise and sent a full statement of the affairs of the Adelsverein in Texas to Mayor Schmidt of Bremen, requesting publication. This was done and had the desired effect. Several of the governments took notice of the accusations made in the article and demanded an explanation from the directorate of the Adelsverein, which resulted in the opening of a credit of $60,000 to von Meusebach. Count Castell was very indignant over the action taken by his agent, Klaener, but the tenseness of the situation was relieved. On June 10, 1846, Castell addressed the following letter to Commissioner General von Meusebach:

"The letter of Mr. Klaener, addressed to the Mayor of Bremen, Mr. Schmidt, and published in the papers, has made the worst impression. It has been communicated to the governments, who now call for an explanation. It states that sickness and death prevail at Indianola and New Braunfels, and that the company does not come up to its promise to remove the immigrants upwards. We would have risked everything if we could not say that we have acted immediately, as soon as we heard how matters stood."

Regarding this credit von Meusebach says: "The letter of advice of this credit of $60,000 from the banker in Germany was dated July 14, 1846; the letter of advice of our New Orleans banker for the same amount was dated August 17, and arrived at New Braunfels on the seventh of September, 1846. If the same amount had been sent one year before, on September, 1845, when the money was due, or over due, probably the most, if not all of the inconveniences, troubles and misfortunes would have been avoided."

Nothing could arraign the Adelsverein more severely than this simple statement.

Many of the immigrants, coming in 1846, heard on board of the emigrant vessels of the piteous conditions of the colonists at New Braunfels, and those who had sufficient means for self support rather sacrificed their contract with the Adelsverein, than risking their lives in the infested colony of the Verein. Some, like J. Frederick, remained in Galveston; others, among them the families of Bering and Cabanis, came to Houston, while some went to Industry, Cat Spring and LaGrange. Of these early pioneers some are still among us at this writing, namely, Messrs. August and Conrad Bering, Hermann Rudolf Cabanis and his two sisters, Mrs. Emma Harde, widow of the late Louis Harde, and Mrs. Agnes Schmidt, widow of August Schmidt, formerly of Houston, but lately of Brooklyn, N. Y., where he died last November at the patriarchal age of 83 years.

CHAPTER XVIII.
Last Effort of the Adelsverein in Colonization.

It has been demonstrated in the preceding chapters that up to the close of the year 1846 none of the immigrants had yet reached the promised land of the Adelsverein. No white man had yet put his foot on the ground of this new Canaan, and the Comanches were still in undisputed and undisturbed possession of it. In the last months of 1846 a "Doctor" Schubert, who had been appointed colonial director at Fredericksburg through recommendation of H. F. Fisher, had organized an expedition for reconnoitering the unknown territory of the grant, expecting to win the laurels of being the first explorer of that country. He bravely advanced to the banks of the Llano River, but although he had a self-constructed, formidable looking cannon with his army of invasion, he did not dare to cross the river; and, without firing a shot, he returned to Fredericksburg, thus imitating the historic king who marched up the hill with 20,000 men, and then marched down again.

To von Meusebach the courageous explorer then made a report that access to the colonial grant was impossible, because the country beyond the Llano River was filled with hostile and savage Indians. Such a report, although spurious and unfounded, von Meusebach could not permit to go abroad unchallenged, and he, therefore, determined at once to go personally to the grant and make some arrangements with the Indians, satisfactory to both parties. It may seem strange that this was not done prior to 1847, but we must not forget that von Meusebach, since his arrival in Texas in April, 1845, had been confronted with the herculean task of providing provisions, transportation and lodgings for thousands of colonists with almost no funds on hand, and had to travel constantly between Galveston, Houston, Nassau, Indianola, New Orleans and New Braunfels to collect sufficient means to keep the immigrants, intrusted to his care, from starvation. In the meantime, von Meusebach had opened a road to the Pedernales River, and in May, 1846, had founded Fredericksburg, as the second relay station to reach the grant.

Now he set out in January, 1847, with three wagons, an interpreter and only 45 men toward the Llano River, which he crossed at the mouth of Beaver Creek, and thus entered as the first the lands of the Fisher and Miller land concession. With this expedition went Dr. Ferdinand Roemer, a geologist from Bonn, Rhenish-Prussia, who later published a meritorious scientific work on the "Cretacious formation of the Mountains of West Texas," (Bonn, 1852), and another book, "Texas," containing a detailed history of the early German immigration to Texas (Bonn, 1849).

The first meeting between von Meusebach and the Indians occurred a few days after he had entered their territory, at a place where the United States later established Fort Mason and where the city of Mason now stands. There the first council was held between von Meusebach and the Comanche Chief, Ketemoszy, in which the latter promised to arrange a meeting of the "White Chief" with the great chiefs of the Comanches a few days later on the banks of the San Saba River. This council took place as arranged and lasted several days. Von Meusebach here had an opportunity to display his courage and presence of mind. When he and his companions approached the Comanches, their chief demanded that as a token of good faith the "white brothers" should discharge their firearms. Without hesitating a moment, Meusebach fired his rifle in the air and his followers did the same. Then the Comanches, who were all armed with heavy American rifles, fired their arms likewise in the air, and thus a sound feeling of mutual confidence was established from the outset. At this meeting von Meusebach laid before the Indian chiefs his plans, and finally the agreement was reached that the council of peace between himself and all the chiefs of the Comanches should be held at the next full moon on the banks of the lower San Saba River. A more detailed account of this momentous meeting will be contained in a succeeding chapter.

While Meusebach was conferring with the Comanches at the council mentioned above, Major Neighbors arrived, dispatched as a courier by Governor Henderson, to urge Meusebach to recross the Llano, as the Comanches had been instigated to hostilities against the Americans by the Mexicans. Meusebach refused to return before his mission was accomplished and engaged Major Neighbors, who had been an Indian agent for the Lipans under the Republic of Texas, to remain with him during his stay in the Indian country. As agreed upon, the council of peace was held at the next full moon on the San Saba River, about 25 miles from its confluence with the Colorado River. A treaty was made with the head chiefs of the Comanches, Buffalo Hump, Santa Anna and Mopechucope, and their warriors, by which the Comanches agreed neither to disturb the surveyors of the Adelsverein nor molest any of the colonists, while Meusebach promised them $3000 worth of presents.

Thus the land was at last opened to colonization, and soon the settlements of Castell, Leiningen, Meerholz and Bettina were established. Bettina, named after the well known authoress, Bettina von Arnim, was the product of an enterprise of 40 college and university men who had formed the so-called "Society of Forty" at Darmstadt in 1847, for the purpose of establishing in Texas, removed from the turmoil of the world, a colony on strictly communistic principles, as an example for the ideal state of the future. These idealists soon experienced the difference between the roseate theories of communistic principles of the utopian order and the practical execution of these promising plans on the prairie lands of Texas. The life of a Texas pioneer was quite different from what these university men had imagined and the Ciceronian "otium cum dignitate procul negotiis" ("rest with dignity far from business troubles") did not materialize. Disillusioned, but not disheartened, they left their "buen retiro" one by one, and their abandoned log cabins were in turn occupied by German farmers, who successfully tilled the ground and became prosperous, where the scientific men had failed.

Among the founders of Bettina were some notable men, Gustav Schleicher, later a prominent Congressman; Jacob Kuechler, commissioner of the General Land Office from 1869-1875; Dr. Ferdinand Herff, for a long time the acknowledged foremost physician in Texas, who died on March 18, 1912, in San Antonio at the advanced age of 91 years, and Herman Spies, the last commissioner general of the Adelsverein. Dr. William Hermes of LaGrange was the youngest member of this party of pioneers, being only 18 years old when he first came to Texas in 1847. In 1851 he returned to Germany for the purpose of studying medicine and, after having finished his studies, came back to Texas. He is now, at the ripe old age of 85 years, the only surviving member of these venturous spirits.

While none of the four settlements mentioned above, except Bettina and Castell, were actually on lands belonging to the Fisher and Miller grant, they were very close to it, and the nearest points to the grant ever reached by the colonization project of the Adelsverein. In the course of time three of the settlements were abandoned for various reasons and only Castell, in Llano County, a village of about 200 inhabitants, has survived.

CHAPTER XIX.
Expedition of von Meusebach to the Comanche Territory and His Treaty With the Indians.

In the preceding chapter brief mention was made of von Meusebach's expedition to the territory between the Colorado, Llano and San Saba Rivers, where the land of Fisher and Miller's grant was situated. This expedition, consisting of 45 men, including three American surveyors, well armed and provisioned, set out from Fredericksburg on January 22, 1847. One of the five Mexicans of the party, who had lived many years among the Comanches, having been kidnaped as a child, served as a guide and interpreter. The expedition under personal command of von Meusebach advanced slowly to the Llano River, reaching its banks on January 21. There a party of six Shawnee Indians was encountered, who were on one of their extensive hunting expeditions. These Shawnees from Arkansas were semi-civilized and friendly. They understood English and von Meusebach succeeded in engaging three of them to accompany his expedition as hunters. Their engagement proved quite fortunate, as neither the German members of the exploring party, nor the Mexicans were successful in hunting the deer, bears or antelopes that were plentiful in the prairies and undergrowth, while the Shawnees now brought several of these animals to camp almost every day.

After crossing the Llano River on February 1 the party had entered the territory proper of the Comanches and had to advance very cautiously, always prepared to meet a sudden and unexpected attack by the Indians, who, as the Shawnees declared, were constantly following and watching von Meusebach and his little band, though invisible to them. Great care had to be observed in the selection and preparing of the night camps, and it was with some difficulty that a proper place could always be found, which provided shelter against the sharp north wind and at the same time protection against an Indian attack. When a suitable spot had been found the eight tents of the company were pitched in a semi-circle and the openings closed by the wagons, while from six to eight fires were kept burning all night in the enclosure, four men being constantly on guard duty. In the flickering light of the camp fires the different costumes, physiognomies and actions of the Mexicans, Indians, Germans and Americans presented a rather picturesque appearance. It was a motley crowd that had ventured into this unexplored country to prepare ways and means for its settlement, and it was also very doubtful if the Comanches would look upon the intrusion into their favorite hunting grounds in a friendly spirit.

On the morning of February 5 eight Comanches were seen riding toward the camp, carrying a white flag. The Mexican Lorenzo was sent by von Meusebach to meet them. Their leader, who said that he was Chief Ketemoszy, inquired solemnly after the chief of the pale faces. Von Meusebach then rode toward them and was informed that the Indians were a deputation of their tribe and wished to hear about the intentions of the white chief and his followers. If they had entered the land of the Comanches with a friendly purpose, all would be well; if they had come to fight, the Indians were ready. Then von Meusebach told the Indians through a Shawnee interpreter that he and his people had nothing but friendly designs in coming to the Comanches' land. They had come from far across the great water and had built two cities in the neighborhood, where the Indians would be received with the same hospitality that he expected from them now. Ketemoszy answered that he would instantly inform the other Indian chiefs of what he had heard, and would call them to meet in council at the next full moon, when a solemn treaty of peace could be arranged. After Ketemoszy and his braves had been treated to an ample repast, of which they partook with evident relish and great appetite, the Indians left, promising to return on the next day, in order to escort von Meusebach and his party to their village. They were true to their promise, and on February 7 the village of the Comanches was reached, situated near the San Saba River, on the slope of a hill, from the summit of which a large white flag was waving a friendly welcome.

Five hunderd Indian warriors, all on horseback, were drawn up in a long line in front of the wigwams with the squaws and children, also on horseback, on the left wing. Von Meusebach was requested to advance with only a few companions, which he did, being met midways between the two parties by as many Indians. After a ceremonious greeting and handshaking, preceded by the firing of all their rifles in the air, as a token of good faith, von Meusebach was invited to enter the village with his whole company as guests of the red men. They remained there during the day, but for the night they prudently removed their camp to the opposite bank of the river under pretext of better grazing ground for their horses. Despite this precaution three of their best horses had mysteriously disappeared during the night, and it required the greatest firmness on the part of von Meusebach to induce their hosts to "find" the strayed animals and return them to their rightful owners. He knew that if he did not insist on the return of the stolen horses, nothing would be safe from the thieving Indians and that the success and probably the very existence of his expedition would be placed in jeopardy. Meusebach's determination made a strong impression upon the Comanches and had the desired effect. The horses were found and returned, and the Indians received some presents in acknowledgement of their diligent search. The expedition remained near the Comanche village several days and was met there by Major Neighbors, as stated in the preceding chapter. On the 10th of February the expedition advanced further into the wilderness and was met on the 12th by emissaries of Santana (Santa Anna), the greatest chief of the Comanches, who also wished to be informed about its intentions in invading the red men's territory. His inquisitiveness being satisfied through the receipt of some presents, von Meusebach, with 14 companions, set out on a further exploration, wishing to reach the old Spanish fort, San Saba, leaving the remainder of his party in their camp and instructing the three American surveyors to make a survey of the surrounding country.

On the 18th of February the Spanish fort was reached. Although in ruins, the walls were still standing to a height of nearly 20 feet, showing that the fort had been 280 feet long and 260 feet wide, containing a great number of small apartments, presumably the living rooms of the former garrisons. The intrepid explorers remained two days at the old fort, during which time Dr. Roemer, the geologist, who had accompanied the expedition, collected various minerals and numerous specimens of petrified plants and animals. Then von Meusebach marched back and was met on February 27 by Indian scouts, who led him and his party to the large Indian village, where, on March 1, the great council of peace between him and the Comanches was to take place.

In this council about 20 Indian chiefs participated, of which Mopechucope (Old Owl), Santana and Pochanaquarhip (Buffalo Hump) were the most prominent. At the time of the midday sun they all arrived at the prearranged meeting place, sitting down in solemn silence on buffalo skins spread out in a wide circle around the campfire, on the embers of which the pipe of peace was to be lighted. Von Meusebach opened this momentous meeting with the following address, which was translated by the Indian interpreter, Jim Shaw, who had arrived with Major Neighbors.

(Translation of a report published in the Magazin für Literatur des Auslandes, 1847.)

My Brethren:

I have come a long way to see you and to smoke the pipe of peace with you. I hope you will listen to the words that I am going to speak to you, for they are words of truth and sincerity, as it is the German's custom. My father's people, which are a martial people, brave and well armed, as you have seen, sent me out and I came with part of my people from far away from across the great waters; we have joined the Americans, they are our brothers, and we all live now under the same great father, the President.

You have lately made peace with the chiefs of that great father. That you may learn to know my people, your present neighbors, and live with them as brothers, I want to consult with you and make a special treaty of peace. Many of my countrymen live near the water that you call Guadaloupe, and many more near another river that we call Pedernales. There they live close together in tents, huts and houses. Now, I intend to come with part of my people to the Llano and there make our homes forever. My countrymen are industrious and thrifty and know how to win from the earth many things that you like to eat and they will always have plenty for themselves and their brothers. But few who cultivate the soil, like to chase the fleeing deer or to kill the buffalo. We do not fear war, but we prefer peace, and if you are willing to wander with our people on the white path of peace, it will gladden the hearts of our wives and warriors, and we then wish that you should abandon the red warpath and tread on the path that is white and visit our people, our cities, villages and wigwams. When we are friends, we shall always share our meals with you, whenever you come to us hungry. If you choose the path of peace with us, you will always receive corn, white flour, sweet sugar and the brown water (coffee), also meat of different kind, and you can exchange for it your skins, horses, and mules, and your squaws and children will know where to receive that, which will gladden their hearts, when they are hungry.

I now make the following proposition:

1. My countrymen have the permission to go and travel where they please, and no harm must be done to them, but you must protect them everywhere. On the other hand, your people can come to our wigwams and cities without fear and can go wherever they please and shall be protected as long as they wander on the white path.

2. You the chiefs, and your people will assist us and report to us, when bad men and redfaces of other tribes steal our horses or intend other felonies, and we shall do the same, when you are attacked.

3. I am going to send men with the thing that steals the land (compasses), as the red men call it, and will survey the whole country of the San Saba as far as the Concho and other waters, so that we may know the boundaries where we can go and till the soil. And if you are willing after consultation with your warriors, to make this treaty, then I will give you and your squaws many presents, or equal them with the white pieces of metal, that we call dollars, and give you as many as one thousand and more of them.

But I do not propose this treaty in order to drive you from your hunting grounds. My people are going to build their wigwams where there is the proper soil for the raising of corn and other plants and we shall dwell and live together like brothers, for it is but little of the land that we are going to occupy, and much will remain for you and your constant abodes. You do neither grow corn nor do you raise cattle or domestic animals, but live by hunting, striking your tents, made of buffalo skins, today in one place, tomorrow in another. When the buffalo has gone northward, and the fleet deer deep into the forest, when you cannot kill any more game with bow and arrow, when the grass is wizen, when your horses have lost flesh and the north wind confines you in your wigwams, then come to my people and exchange what you have for the necessities of life. Many of you are often now hungry for days —then you will always have plenty to eat, for my people will raise on little ground more than we need for our support.

I cannot tell now exactly where I shall erect the wigwams and houses of my people, but it will be near or at the water, that you call Llano. I wish you to consider well what I say.

When my people has lived with you for some time, and when we know each other better, then it may happen that some wish to marry. Soon our warriors will learn your language. If they then wish to wed a girl of your tribe, I do not see any obstacle, and our people will be so much better friends.

When we agree on this treaty, I shall go and fetch the presents and will be ready to sign the treaty solemnly, at the latest when the disk of the moon has rounded twice. I hope that you will agree with me, and I conjure the earth, our common mother, that I have not spoken with a divided tongue. I have no more to say to my brethren. I hear what they are going to reply.

On the 2d day of March, in another council meeting, Chief Mopechucope gave the following answer:

"My friend and father has come a long way to see me. I have heard his words and believe and trust to what he said yesterday at the meeting to the chiefs. The hearts of my people are gladdened after having listened to my father's words.

"I formerly saw a black streak under my finger nail, but today I see that it is white. My heart rejoices to see the people that came from so far over the great water to see us.

"I have spoken to my people. I have consulted with the warriors and with the old men. We shall abandon the war path and travel on the white path of peace, as my father proposed yesterday, and I will do my utmost that we remain forever on this path, after the treaty has been made.

"But I perceive something that is not dear to my heart, when you now are going to build your wigwams at the water called the Llano. I know that the people, that calls itself Texans, want to erect a barrier between us and the palefaces and I must speak first with the Comanches farther away, because I do not want to promise anything and break my word afterwards. When the grass is growing again, the Comanches will meet and I hope that I can remove all difficulties. My intention is to walk the path of peace under all circumstances on this side of the Brazos River. I have no more to say."

To this von Meusebach answered at once as follows:

"My brother has spoken—I have listened to his words and weighed them. The hearts of our women and children will be gladdened when they listen to the words of peace uttered by my brother. He is not opposed to our building our wigwams at the banks of the water called Llano. My brother will walk the white path of peace and he will speak with the other Comanches and they will listen to the words of their chief.

"My brother speaks of a barrier between the redmen and the palefaces. I do not disdain my red brethren because their skin is darker, and I do not think more of the white people because their complexion is lighter. If our father, the President, wishes to draw this line of distinction, he may do so, I shall not see it, because we are brothers and will live together like brothers. My people has nothing to do with the redmen on the other side of the Brazos. We do not wish to make a treaty of peace with them but only with the brave Comanches, my brethren. I have spoken."

Chief Mopechucope replied:

"My heart is glad to hear what my brother said. I shall come with my people to the place you call Fredericksburg, as soon as the moon has been full the second time. When you are ready to receive us, send us the messenger whom we can trust, to have been sent by you, and we shall come to sign the treaty of peace as you have promised. This is my speech."

Then Chief Santa Anna spoke as follows:

"My brothers, we have listened to your words. Our people will do what we, the highest chiefs, are going to decide upon and ordain. We hope that all is true what you have said. This will be proven when it comes to the ratification of the treaty and to the presents. I believe you and your people are friendly disposed toward us. I have seen our great father in Washington. We have made a good treaty of peace with him. I hope that the treaty we are about to make with you and your people, will be just as good and sound. I have not forgotten our great father's speech. It is engraved in my heart and I see him every morning when I awake, as he was in Washington and as he spoke to me. I hope, my German brother is like my great father. I hope he has a wide, white heart, like my father, the President, for all his children. My brother will walk the white path of peace and keep it with my people, as the path of peace has been kept until now with my great father. And the white path will be wide and lead to his door, to his heart, and to the hearts of the German people, so that my people can use it and remain on it without fear of treachery. I have spoken."

Chief Buffalo-Hump remarked: "Do not believe that I

am opposed to anything, because I have not spoken. My friends have spoken. My chiefs and my warriors have consulted. My people have listened. I agree with all that Mopechucope and Santana have said. I have spoken."

This ended the important council and later, as agreed upon, the treaty of peace between the German pioneers and the Comanches was ratified at Fredericksburg. Through this treaty the land concession acquired by the Adelsverein had at last become of some value to the German immigrants. Before von Meusebach's treaty with the Indians it had been but a negligible quantity, and the more so because the Government of Texas had declined to render any assistance to the Verein in its endeavor to reach a friendly understanding with the Indians, who had absolute control of the land.

We cannot but admire the courage of von Meusebach, who, with a few followers, fearlessly penetrated into the unknown territory, but must also give due credit to the able and skilled manner in which he dealt with the ferocious and warlike Comanches, inducing them to sign a treaty, which opened the hitherto forbidden land to German settlements.

The opening of this vast territory of 3,000,000 acres to civilization and cultivation is without doubt the most important pioneer work of the Germans in Texas, and could only be accomplished through the absolute confidence the Indians placed in the Germans' promises and pledges. The Lone Star State owes a debt of gratitude to the early German settlers of the San Saba territory, and their courage and perseverance deserve proper mention in all Texas histories.

While the Indians trusted the pledges of the Germans implicitly, and were treated with every consideration possible by the German settlers, there were, nevertheless a number of conflicts between them and roving bands of redskins, who, on their foraging expeditions, laid their hands on everything in sight, and horses and cattle had to be carefully guarded. Of the different Indian attacks and depredations, the following deserve to be mentioned, viz.:

In the fall of 1846, a camp of immigrants was suddenly attacked on the banks of the Guadaloupe River, and in the fight that followed, several of the immigrants were killed. In 1847, Lieutenant von Wrede and two companions were treacherously killed by Indians between Austin and Piedernales, and in the same year several settlers were wounded while working in their gardens at Fredericksburg. The Comanches remained friendly while their Chief Santana, who was a staunch friend of the Germans, lived; but after he had died in 1848, a victim of cholera, and especially after the arrival of United States troops, who established Fort Mason, the Comanches gradually became as unreliable friends as the Lipans. In 1855, Herman Runge, son of Dr. Runge of Sisterdale, was killed and scalped in a field of A. Dresel's farm by several Comanches, who also stole a number of horses from Dr. Runge's farm. A pursuit to avenge the death of young Runge was futile, as the marauding Indians had a start of almost twelve hours. On February 13, 1863, Heinrich Arhelger was killed by a band of Indians near Fredericksburg after a valiant fight on his side, during which he killed one Indian with a bullet from his revolver and wounded several others. The Indians must have beaten a hasty retreat, as they did not even scalp the victim of their villainous attack. In October, 1863, Conrad and Heinrich Meckel of Fredericksburg were murdered by a band of Indians on the road between Loyal Valley and Cherry Springs, while they were resting, and probably had fallen asleep. They were robbed of everything, but not scalped. In the spring of 1864, Rudolph Fischer, the twelve-year-old son of Gottlieb Fischer of Fredericksburg, was kidnaped. Twelve years later he returned and tried to lead again a civilized life, but he had been Indianized to such an extent, and the broad prairies of West Texas had so enthralled him, that in less than one year he discarded his civilian garb, dressed in Indian fashion, painted his face red and rode off, never to return.

On February 8, 1865, four Indians waylaid Miss Anna Metzger, 20 years old, and her younger sister Katherine, 13 years old, on their way from Fredericksburg to their father's farm, north of the city, and after having assaulted both girls, they lifted them on their horses to carry them off. The older girl, trying to escape in the bushes that flanked the road, was killed by an arrow and horribly mutilated by the savages. The younger sister, after some months of hard life among the Indians, was taken by her captors to the Indian agent to be offered to him for sale, it then being the custom that the Indian agents bought the white captives of the Indians, the military forces not being strong enough to effectively cope against the numerous Indian tribes and force them to return their white preys. The price the Indians asked for the liberation of the girl seemed too high to the agent and the bargain was not concluded on the first day. During the night, the girl escaped the vigilance of her captors and hid in a nearby cornfield, from where she was released on the following afternoon by the agent and returned to her distracted parents.

In August of the same year, Mr. Heinrich Kensing, a farmer on Beaver Creek, Gillespie County, returning home with his wife from a visit at his brother's farm, on the Squaw Creek, was attacked by six Comanche Indians on horseback, and he and his wife were both murdered and scalped.

In the year 1867, four women were taken by Comanches from a blockhouse in which they had sought refuge during the absence of their husbands; one of them was assaulted and killed, the other three being carried off by the savages and nothing was heard of them any more. In 1868 or 1869, Hermann Lehmann was kidnaped by Comanches in Mason

County. He remained several years among them, but returned to his widowed mother and became a prosperous farmer.

Several other atrocities and murders were committed by the redskins until late in the seventies, but in the whole, the German pioneers of West Texas had not to suffer as much as the early settlers in Nebraska, Minnesota and Dakota, a result of the fair treatment that was invariably accorded the Indians by the Germans.

CHAPTER XX.
Collapse of the Adelsverein.

The expedition of von Meusebach to the Llano-San Saba territory and his treaty with the Indians were his last official acts of importance as commissioner general of the Adelsverein. Before leaving New Braunfels on this expedition he had sent to the directorate with his report of January 19, 1847, his irrevocable resignation. This was, probably reluctantly, accepted, and on July 20, 1847, von Meusebach turned the office over to his successor, Hermann Spiess. For over two years von Meusebach had conducted the affairs of the Adelsverein in Texas under the most trying conditions in an able manner, and although he sometimes was arbitrary in his actions and decisions, he unquestionably deserves the highest credit and appreciation for his unselfishness, determination, prompt action and personal courage, qualifications that enabled him to be of real service to the thousands of immigrants thrust upon his care by the senseless haste with which the emigrants were sent to Texas by the Adelsverein.

Under the auspices of the Verein a total of 7380 immigrants had come to Texas, viz.:

In 1844.................. 700 immigrants
In 1845..................4,304 immigrants
In 1846..................2,376 immigrants

Most immigrants, arriving at Galveston in 1847, numbering 8000, according to Franz Loeher in his "History and Conditions of the Germans in America" (Cincinnati and Leipzig, 1849), did not come any more under the auspices of the Adelsverein, the activity of which had practically ceased with the end of the year 1846.

The unavoidable catastrophe was on hand. It was the

German Element in Texas 109

logical sequence of the inconceivably childish credulity with which Count Castell, the managing director of the Adelsverein, had fallen victim to the shrewd schemes of Bourgeois and Fisher, his utter lack of business ability and the total ignorance of conditions existing in Texas. Furthermore the capital of $80,000 was entirely inadequate for an enterprise of the magnitude of the hazy colonization project of the Adelsverein, an enterprise that would have required a capital of perhaps $1,000,000 to make it successful. And even then it might have been a failure after the purchase of the Fisher and Miller grant and under such incompetent management at that of Count Castell. When on July 22, 1844, he signed the agreement with H. F. Fisher, which was nothing but a simple assumption of the rights and obligations of Fisher and Miller, he believed that he had actually purchased several millions of acres of land, and without knowing anything about that land, he informed the public on December 11, 1844, that the Adelsverein had acquired these extraordinary fertile lands on the right banks of the Colorado River. It seems that Count Castell neither made himself acquainted with the wording of the contract between the Adelsverein and Fisher and Miller, nor that he had any knowledge whatever of the colonization laws of Texas, whither he intended to send thousands of families.

Count Waldeck had advised against colonization on an extensive plan, and had declared the Fisher and Miller grant an undesirable location, as it was almost 300 miles from the sea coast, but his sound advice was not heeded and now, after the short colonization period of less than three years, and an accumulated debt of several hundred thousand dollars, the commissioner general in Texas was informed that the Adelsverein was unable to fulfill its promises and obligations, and that the colonists at New Braunfels and Fredericksburg had to get along the best way they could. The bubble had burst and the hopes of several thousand men, women and children, who had implicitly trusted the words and pledges of princes and lords, were ruthlessly shattered.

Great was the consternation and great the misery when in the summer of 1847 the announcement was made by Commissioner Spiess in both settlements that the Adelsverein was hopelessly bankrupt, and that the colonists were left to their own resources. Not one of these unfortunate people would have remained at either New Braunfels or Fredericksburg, if he had possessed the means of returning to the fatherland that he had left only a short time ago with fine hopes and under such glittering promises. But it proved well for them that they were forced to remain at these primitive settlements. After the first outbursts of despair and agony were over, they all set determinedly to work, and by hard and persistent labor in cultivating their ten acres, and living on the barest necessities of life for several years, they not only succeeded in establishing a firm existence for themselves and their families, but in course of time made New Braunfels and Fredericksburg the garden spots of Texas. These German settlers, toiling incessantly under adverse conditions for civilization, performed a most noble pioneer work, and are entitled to our highest admiration. Texas would not be what it is today, if these brave men and women of the forties of the last century had not unflinchingly and fearlessly taken upon themselves the dangerous and onerous task of clearing this West Texas wilderness and preparing for the farmer a vast agricultural region, where, before their arrival the Indians hunted and large buffalo herds roamed undisturbed over the boundless prairies.

When the collapse of the Adelsverein was announced in Texas the farm Nassau, in Fayette County, became the bone of contention. "Dr." Schubert, the colonial director of Fredericksburg, whose real name was Strohberg, and who was a bankrupt tobacco merchant from Cassel, where

H. F. Fisher, who recommended him to von Meusebach, was also born, then believed the time ripe to get possession of this valuable plantation of 4428 acres. Some time in 1846 Schubert had obtained a lease for eight years on the farm Nassau from von Meusebach. In 1847, H. Wilke, the lessee, threw up his contract on account of sickness, and then Adolph Benner, later for many years postmaster at New Braunfels, was appointed superintendent of the farm, because Schubert had not given or could not give any security for payment of the rent for the plantation. But he was determined to get possession of it by any means.

One morning he appeared at the farm with two witnesses and demanded surrender of all the property to him on account of the contract made previously with von Meusebach. According to instructions Benner refused to turn over the property and Schubert left the place. A few days later he reappeared with two Americans, one of whom represented himself as the Sheriff of Fayette County and read an English paper to Benner, stating that it was an order from the County Court at LaGrange, demanding the surrender of the farm and all implements to Dr. Schubert. Benner, as well as his assistant, Ernest Soergel, who both had been in Texas only a few months, and did not understand English, now complied with the demand, and vacated the property. Coming to LaGrange, they were greatly surprised to hear, that the court there had not issued any such order and that the whole affair was a trick of Schubert to get possession of the farm. He had been successful, and for some months remained in undisputed possession, keeping a small American bodyguard for the protection of himself and his property, among them, the two men, J. Bostick and G. W. Breeding, who had impersonated the sheriff and his deputy.

After an unsuccessful attempt made by Commissioner General Spiess on October 28, 1847, to oust Schubert from

Nassau by force, during which an American named Summers, and a German painter, by name of Rohrdorf, were killed, the claims of Schubert were finally compromised by paying $4000, after which he returned to Germany. Later he published several sensational novels about Texas life under the nom de plume "Armand," that excelled in the description of the most thrilling adventures and bloody combats.

Then Otto von Roeder was appointed superintendent of the farm Nassau. In 1849 he bought the property from the bankrupt Adelsverein for $18,000, which amount the Adelsverein owed him for corn and flour, and sold part of the lands in small tracts to new German settlers. Two years later, in 1851, execution of a judgment of $150 against the defunct Adelsverein was ordered by the court at LaGrange and as von Roeder steadfastly refused to pay this, the remaining property of farm Nassau was sold at sheriff's sale to Mr. James Chandler for 4 cents the acre. The appeal of von Roeder was carried to the United States Supreme Court. This tribunal rendered its final decision in 1865, in which it declared that the Adelsverein had never been the legal owner of farm Nassau, as it was neither incorporated in Germany, nor in the United States. The judgment of the lower court was confirmed and von Roeder lost all.

Herman Spiess, who had been tried for the murder of Captain Summers at LaGrange in the fall of 1848 and acquitted by a jury composed of none but Americans, remained commissioner general of the Adelsverein in Texas until 1852, but had very little to do, except representing the Verein in litigation before the courts of Fayette, Bexar, and Harris Counties. He was replaced in 1852 by former Lieutenant Bene, who was the last official representative of the Adelsverein in Texas. After another year of practical inactivity the Verein withdrew finally from Texas, by assigning on September 13, 1853, all its property in

Texas, and all rights derived from the colonization grant to its Texas creditors. This was the ignominious finale of the ostentatious colonization enterprise of German nobility, conceived in arrogance and carried out in the most incompetent manner imaginable.

After the actual collapse of the Adelsverein Fisher and Miller tried to reap the profits of the land grant that they had sold to the Adelsverein for themselves. On August 23, 1851, they appeared before Granville H. Sherwood, commissioner for the Fisher and Miller grant, and stated under oath that the German Immigration Company (the Adelsverein), had introduced and settled in Texas 1600 families and 1000 single men, and therefore was entitled to 160 sections of 640 acres each and 100 half sections of 320 acres, a total of 134,400 acres, as the stipulated premium for the settling of European immigrants. It will be remembered that Fisher and Miller were represented by three votes in the "Colonialrat" of the Adelsverein, but in 1851, this committee had ceased to exist for several years. Despite this fact, Fisher and Miller had procured judgment, which ordered that the certificates and title to these 134,400 acres should be made out in their name. Commissioner Sherwood did so, but the Commissioner of the General Land Office refused to issue the patents for the land demanded. When the petition of Fisher and Miller to legalize their claim came up in the House of Representatives in the spring of 1852, the Hon. Sam Maverick of Bexar County, opposed it vehemently in a forceful speech that concluded with the following words:

"They (Fisher and Miller) say that they have judgment for their claim; it is a snap judgment secured in a dark corner; it is a fraud, a fraud!" The House then rejected the petition. (Meusebach. Ans. p. 9.)

CHAPTER XXI.
Criticism of the Adelsverein.

Much has been written about the Adelsverein. Dr. F. Kapp, A. Siemering, J. von Meusebach, William von Rosenberg, L. F. Lafrentz, A. Eickhoff, Alvin H. Soergel, Dr. Roemer and G. G. Benjamin have all contributed to its pathetic history. They all are unanimous in their strong condemnation of its methods, but some of them vary greatly about the motives, that induced German princes and noblemen to engage in an emigration and colonization project, while some of the authors mentioned above do not touch the interesting, but intricate question of the motives of the Adelsverein at all.

Eickhoff simply calls the enterprise "A tragedy of errors," while Dr. Kapp, who visited Texas in 1852, reaches the following conclusion: "I am far from accusing this noble association, as has been often done, of an intentional deception of the emigrants, or of a speculation for monetary gain. This accusation is absurd, because men of the exalted position of the founders of the Adelsverein, and among them very wealthy princes, would have found much nearer and safer places for speculation, if they really wished to engage in it, than the then uncivilized Texas. Aside from this, considering the most honorable, public spirited and unblemished character of the members of the Verein, I am firmly convinced of their philanthropic intentions. As they spoke in their public announcements, men only can speak who are firmly convinced of the purity and unselfishness of their enterprise." (F. Kapp, "Aus und über America," Berlin, 1876.)

A. Siemering, on the other hand, asserts that the Adelsverein was organized and manipulated in the interest of England and was paid by the English Government to direct German immigration to Texas, for the purpose of preventing annexation to the United States and abolishing slavery in Texas, thus erecting a barrier against the spreading of slavery, as well as against the extension of the United States.

I am constrained to differ with both Kapp and Siemering. The latter's assumption that the Adelsverein was an agency of British diplomacy and was subsidized by England, is made without any basis of truth and unsubstantiated by any documentary evidence. Siemering was an inveterate revolutionist, who hated the very name of royalty or prince, and this bitter aversion led him to impute sinister motives to any of their actions. His imputation does not deserve serious consideration.

It is true that England wished to prevent annexation of Texas to the United States and that the English Government and the strong abolitionist party in England favored the abolishment of slavery as much in Texas as anywhere, but when the Adelsverein started its colonizatin movement in the fall of 1844, all chances of England to get control of Texas by advancing a loan to the Republic and making a commercial treaty with it, had vanished through the election of Polk to the presidency of the United States in 1844, which meant the final annexation of Texas. Before the news of Polk's election spread in Texas, Anson Jones, opposed to annexation and leaning toward England, which had dropped its former demand for abolishment of slavery in Texas in return of England's recognition of the independence of Texas, had been elected President of the Republic and for a short time it seemed as if England would yet receive control of Texas and the Gulf of Mexico. Prince Solms, who was then at Galveston, sent President Jones the following letter, dated December 3, 1844:

"To His Excellency, President Anson Jones.

"Honored Sir: I send you these lines to express my

deep regret that I cannot be present at your inauguration as President of the Republic, but, my emigrants having just arrived, makes my presence at Lavaca Bay imperative. I spoke today with General Duff Green, Consul of the United States in Galveston, and from his words I could instantly interpret the meaning of his mission. He spoke of a threatening attack by Mexico and advises annexation to the United States. It is my duty to inform you, that my last dispatches from Europe apprise me that annexation would mean a possible war between England and the United States. Green shall urge us to a war with Mexico, and promises assistance of the United States.

"I am at your service and ready to visit Santa Anna, or in any other way to act according to your wishes.
"Karl, Prince von Solms."

All European citizens of Texas were against annexation, because they were against slavery and believed this odious institution could be more easily abolished if Texas remained independent, than if it should join the United States.

Captain George Elliot, the English diplomatic agent for Texas, offered an English loan of £5,000,000 sterling and exerted his whole influence against annexation, and as the Oregon question became an important factor at that time, the situation seemed favorable for England's aspirations in regard to Texas. But President Tyler and his Secretary of State, Calhoun, were equal to the occasion and the Gordian knot of the Texas question was settled on the last day of President Tyler's administration, when on March 3, 1845, he signed the joint resolution of Congress authorizing the annexation of Texas. On the same day Calhoun sent a dispatch to Texas, offering the army and navy of the United States to Texas in case of war with Mexico, and the American agents kept up an active agitation, urging the people of Texas "to return to their father's home." In a general election, held on October

13, 1845, the annexation of Texas was almost unanimously ratified, and on February 19, 1846, President Anson Jones handed over the executive authority to Pinckney Henderson, first Governor of the State of Texas.

Thus, the annexation of Texas to the United States, that had dragged for almost ten years, was accomplished and, as demonstrated, above, the Adelsverein could not be of any service to England's aspirations, although its interest lay in the same direction.

An independent Republic of Texas, politically and financially weak, was more favorable, yea, even indispensable, to the purpose of the Adelsverein than the sovereign State of Texas, a member of the powerful United States. The real object of the Adelsverein, as expressed in their first declaration from Biebrich in 1842, was "the purchase and acquisition of lands in the free State of Texas." Through the arbitrary actions of Napoleon, later sanctioned by the Congress of Vienna, many petty principalities in Western Germany had been abolished, and their former sovereign rulers were reduced to simple lords of their private family estates. These estates were entailed by the law of progeniture to fall always to the eldest son or nearest male heir, leaving the other sons and daughters of these deposed princes and landgraves in comparative indigence and dependency. Then Texas arose as the bright star of hope from its unknown darkness through the glowing descriptions of Hecke, Sealsfield, Duden and others, and as these noble lords had but a very dim knowledge of the real conditions in Texas, they readily grasped the idea of procuring estates for their offspring in this land of fabled beauty and grandeur. The philanthropy of which Dr. Kapp speaks, was exclusively directed toward their sons and relatives, for which they desired to establish large estates on which they could live properly as lords and barons. The German immigrants were simply a necessity and the Adelsverein expected that the princes and counts would be able to keep them always in a kind of dependency so that they had some real subjects to rule. This might have been barely possible if Texas had remained an independent republic, but as a sovereign State of the great American Union, Texas was no longer a proper field for aristocratic feudal estates. As soon as it became known in Europe that the annexation of Texas was a foregone conclusion, Prince Solms' mission had come to an end. He was recalled and glad to leave a country, the very air of which seemed to infuse democratic tendencies into former loyal subjects, who had grossly offended the Prince's feelings by hoisting a Texas flag on the square in New Braunfels, while Prince Solms had unfurled the Austrian banner (there being no German flag in 1845) on the Sophienburg.

That the Adelsverein, or its leading director, Count Castell, showed very little consideration for the emigrants, is sufficiently demonstrated by the careless manner in which the financial matters were handled, which for him and the members of the general committee seemed always to be of secondary importance. To one of von Meusebach's many appeals for funds, he briefly answered on March 24, 1846: "The general committee did make the mistake of sending the immigrants, but not the money required for their transportation."

The history of the Adelsverein was not only a tragedy of errors, as Eickhoff says, but a gross and inexcusable deception from beginning to end, probably an unintentional deception, as F. Kapp states, but, nevertheless, a deception that was almost criminal and that points to a very poor development of the intellectual faculties of its leading members.

Some writers state that Count Castell wished to emulate the British East India Company in Texas. This assumption seems almost too far fetched for serious consideration, but, if the Adelsverein and Count Castell should have harbored such an absurd idea, it is only further proof of the haziness of their immature plans. The Adelsverein was the direct opposite of the East India Company. The latter was an organization of shrewd and energetic business men, having a set purpose in mind that was carried out systematically and with an unwavering determination, while the princes and lords of the Adelsverein were as incompetent in business affairs as children and their plans visionary and totally impracticable. Business men were rigorously barred from this association "inter pares." Then the conditions existing in India were entirely different from those in Texas. The East Indies were a country inhabited by more than 150,000,000 people, who enjoyed a certain Oriental civilization, and were ready to buy European manufactured goods in exchange for the rich tropical products of their fertile country, their gold and precious stones, while Texas in 1844 did not have more than 120,000 white inhabitants and otherwise was almost barren of civilization and cultivation. There were no articles of export in Texas besides cotton, and its needs for industrial products of Europe were insignificant.

It is therefore hardly conceivable that the Adelsverein, or Count Castell, even with their limited knowledge of Texas, entertained the plan of a commercial organization, and the plain fact remains that they only hoped to acquire extensive landed estates for their families with the least possible expense. Ottomar von Behr in his book, "'Advice to Immigrants" (Leipzig, 1847), says that "the Adelsverein wished to establish in Texas a feudal State, which would lend money to the settlers, and, by keeping them in a more or less dependent state, they would be treated, in a way, as mere subjects."

To satisfy this desire was the Adelsverein's first and only aim, and on account of a total ignorance of Texas and a stupendous credulity the directorate of the society of noblemen fell an easy prey to scheming promoters, but it is not only subjected to severest criticism for the deplorable inefficiency with which the financial affairs were conducted, but must also be condemned for the wanton sacrifice of hundreds of lives of immigrants who had implicit faith in the pledges and promises of their princes and sovereigns.

Although the Adelsverein had been practically bankrupt since the beginning of 1847, the directorate of this society still continued to make contracts, promising not only land, but also a small block house to each emigrant, but the latter was never furnished, and even the land was generally so far from any organized settlement that many of the prospective settlers preferred to drop their contract with the Adelsverein when they reached Galveston. The diary of C. Groos, grandfather of Hon. C. J. von Rosenberg, LaGrange, shows that he emigrated to Texas in the fall of 1848 under a contract with the Adelsverein, according to which he was to receive 320 acres of good, tillable land and a block house. After his landing at Galveston with his family of eight children, he found that he could neither receive the land nor the house. He therefore went to Fayette County, where he bought a small tract of the farm Nassau from von Roeder, who then was the de facto owner of this farm. Von Roeder gave Groos credit for the $100 paid by the latter to the Adelsverein for free transportation to West Texas and the promised house, and even allowed $40 interest. of the eight children of C. Groos, who arrived in Texas with their father in 1848, three are still living, Mrs. Emilie Giesecke and Adolph Groos of San Antonio and Mrs. Wilhelmina Giesecke, widow of Captain Julius Giesecke, at New Braunfels.

CHAPTER XXII.
The Revolution of 1848 and Its Effects on German Emigration.

In the year 1848 continental Europe experienced another momentous political upheaval. The signal was again given in Paris, where on February 24, Louis Philipp of Orleans, the citizen-king, was forced to abdicate and the republic proclaimed. This was followed in March by a general uprising of the people in Berlin, Vienna and many other cities throughout the German States. "Down with Metternich and his system," was not only the cry of the inhabitants of Vienna, but was shouted aloud by the infuriated masses everywhere in Germany. The Emperor of Austria and the King of Prussia were compelled to grant their people the long promised constitutional government, but the uprising in Baden in 1849 was forcibly put down by Prussian regiments, and the reaction following forced many of the best German patriots who had taken part in the revolution to seek safety in Switzerland, England and America.

This exodus of university professors, literary men, artists and students from every German State was considerably augmented by thousands of mechanics and farmers who were driven from their homes by unbearable administrative ordinances and annoying police surveillance, and "the Forty-eighters," as these immigrants were generally called, were soon to be found in great numbers in New York, Illinois, Ohio, Michigan, Wisconsin, Missouri and Texas. The wave of immigration ran high in 1848 and 1849, and the quota that Texas received did certainly not fall much below the number of immigrants in 1847, when, according to Franz von Loeher, 8000 Germans landed in Galveston. It is impossible to state the accurate number as all shipping lists from 1840-1860 were destroyed in the Galveston storm of 1900.

Most of the German immigrants coming to Texas were peasants and mechanics, but as in the early thirties, so it was in 1848 and 1849, that quite a number of highly educated men were among them. The most noted of them were Dr. Adolf Douay, Dr. E. Runge, Ed Degener, Ottmar von Behr, A. von Westphal, Prof. Rodius, Dr. Ernst Kapp, Julius Dressel, Captain E. B. H. Schneider and Dr. A. Hertzberg. Dr. Douay was the founder of the first German newspaper in San Antonio in 1854, and fearlessly but very uncautously advocated abolition of slavery. When the tension between pro and antislavery parties grew, he was forced to sell his paper and leave the State. Edward Degener represented the Fourth Congressional district of Texas in Washington from 1870-1874, after which he retired from public life, living in San Antonio until his death in 1891, beloved and esteemed by thousands of friends.

Prof. Ernst Kapp, former teacher at the College of Minden, Westphalia, was the author of a scientific "Comparative Geography" and a brother of Dr. Frederick Kapp, mentioned in a preceding chapter. E. B. H. Schneider, one of the founders of the Houston Turnverein in 1854, was captain of the Turner Rifles during the war of secession and was wounded at Galveston at the capture of the sloop Harriet Lane. He died in Houston, where he had lived for 54 years, on January 1, 1903. Except Captain Schneider, all of the men mentioned above had lived for some years at Sisterdale, northwest of San Antonio, that became known as the Latin settlement. Sisterdale, so named from two mountains overlooking the valley and traversed by the Sister Creek, formed by two brooks that run in a parallel direction for miles, is a most beautiful and romantic spot of West Texas. The first house in the valley was built in 1847 by Lieutenant Colonel Zink, who had plotted New Braunfels in 1845, but becoming dissatisfied, had moved westward. Being enthusiastic over the picturesque scenery of Sisterdale, he decided to make the valley his future home and built his block house on Sister Creek near where it empties into the Guadalupe River. He was soon joined by Ottomar von Behr, who erected his home on the western banks of the Guadalupe, on a prominence overlooking the valley, with a magnificent view of the beautiful panorama of hills and dale. Then Edward Degener, Professor Kapp, Dr. Douay, von Westphal, Dr. Runge, von Donop, von Meusebach and other men of culture and means arrived, all of whom were accomplished Greek and Latin scholars, but, except Degener, knew almost nothing about farming. The "Latin Settlement" had been born—a library of the ancient and modern classics was to be found in almost every house and the latest products of literature were eagerly read and discussed at the weekly meetings of these gentlemen farmers at the school house. It sometimes occurred at these meetings that Comanches stood listening gravely at the open door, while one of the Latin farmers was lecturing on the socialistic theories of St. Simon or Fourier. Their social life was most refined and reached its climax when Prince Paul of Wuerttemberg, brother of the reigning King, arrived at Sisterdale. Prince Paul was a naturalist and botanist of note and during his extensive travels had also come to Texas, where he was highly pleased to find real drawing-room conversation on the borders of civilization.

These men of Sisterdale were strict abolitionists and in 1853 organized a political society, the "Freier Verein" (free association), that called a German convention in May, 1854, which assembled at San Antonio. Among the resolutions adopted by this convention was one declaring that "Slavery is an evil and should be abolished." This was in full accord with the sentiments of all Germans in Texas, who, like Sam Houston, in 1861 tried to prevent Texas from joining the secession. In the "San Antonio Zeitung" they had an organ that ably and aggressively advocated their abolitionistic doctrines and during the war between the States the unionistic feeling throughout West Texas was quite pronounced.

The Latin Settlement did not survive the Civil War. Its fame came to an end with the death or removal of its founders. Degener and Dressel were taken to San Antonio in 1862 as prisoners of war, and although soon discharged, did not return to Sisterdale. Von Donop was killed by Indians, Dr. Runge died and Dr. Knapp returned to Germany in 1864. O. von Behr died during a voyage to Germany and others moved to San Antonio or Austin. As in the colony Bettina, so in Sisterdale the places of the literary men were taken by German farmers, and the scientific discussions on the merits of the epics of Virgil and Homer were replaced by the more practical conversations about agricultural requirements.

Many writers of Texas history name Castroville among the early German settlements. This is not proper, because Henry Castro, the founder, was a Frenchman, and his colonists came mainly from Belgium and Alsace, which in 1844 still belonged to France, although most of the Alsatians spoke German and acknowledged to be Germans after the Franco-German war of 1870-1871. Castro's grant was from 25 to 50 miles west of San Antonio in the present counties of Medina, Frio and Uvalde, and its location, although near the Mexican boundary, was, at that time, far better adapted to European colonization than the Fisher and Miller grant, 150 miles north of it. When Prince Solms arrived at San Antonio on July 27, 1844, he at once began negotiations for the purchase of 17 leagues (75,276 acres) of land directly northeast of Castro's grant and owned by a citizen of San Antonio named John McMullen. Castro, whose first colonists had just then arrived at San Antonio, was absent on his grant, looking for a suitable place to establish his first settlement. When he returned to San Antonio on July 31, Prince Solms had started for the land he expected to buy for the German colonists. Before he returned, Castro had contracted with McMullen to colonize his 17 leagues. In his diary Castro writes the following in reference to this transaction: "I understood that if he (Prince Solms) negotiated for the occupation of such a tract of land, my enterprise would be ruined, and, taking advantage of his absence, I entered into negotiations with McMullen and with the assistance of one of our most able and honorable attorneys, Mr. Vanderlip, made a contract with the said John McMullen to colonize his grant on certain conditions. When the Prince returned to San Antonio he certainly was disappointed." Thus the Adelsverein unfortunately was deprived of a most promising opportunity to acquire a large tract of fine farming land, near a city and other settlements and admirably suited for German colonization.

In 1850 the first United States census in Texas was taken. Its figures of the number of Germans in Texas is far from being correct. It gives 8191 inhabitants as having been born in Germany. Under the auspices of the Adelsverein alone there had come to Texas 7380 immigrants, while in 1847, 1848 and 1849 about 15,000 more Germans had arrived, and more than 10,000 from 1830 to 1845. This makes a total of about 33,000 Germans in Texas in 1850. The number of deaths from 1830 to 1850, despite the fearful epidemics at New Braunfels and Fredericksburg in 1846, did certainly not exceed the number of births, as these pioneers had plenty of children. In South and Southwest Texas many Germans lived in every town and city, while numerous settlements were entirely German, and have so remained to the present day.

The Germans comprised one-fifth of the total white population of Texas in 1850. Of these 6000 lived in Eastern Texas, about equally divided between Harris and Galveston Counties; 10,000 were in Central Texas, in Austin, Washington, Fayette, Colorado, Milam, Bastrop, Travis and other counties, while more than 15,000 lived in Western

Texas in the present counties of Comal, Bexar, Gillespie, Medina, Guadaloupe, De Witt, Victoria, Calhoun, Caldwell, Llano, Hays, Kerr and Gonzales. German influence in the development of Texas was very pronounced and can hardly be overestimated. Their intrepidity opened up a heretofore unknown country and in exposed positions they firmly established their settlements and cultivated the virgin soil; they as the first pioneers crossed the rivers and brooks of West Texas and won wide stretches of land from the Indians for the civilization of the white race. Their noble and courageous work should always be properly remembered.

CHAPTER XXIII.
Industrial Establishments of the Early German Settlers and Their Relation to the Anglo-Saxons.

The generation of the twentieth century purchases almost every article or necessity "ready made." Ours is the age of factory products, manufactured by the million in the large and ever-growing industrial establishments of the manufacturing centers and sold in the humblest village everywhere. Sixty years ago this was very different. While, of course, many factories then also existed in the larger cities of the United States, the ready-made article did not control and absorb the entire market as at present. The master mechanic had a chance to work in his own shop, and all articles made by him "to order," bearing a certain stamp of individuality, were vastly preferred to goods with the trademark of some factory. Now the master mechanic, who could once point with pride to the products of his skill and workmanship, has almost disappeared, sacrificed on the altar of the factory-Moloch and trade monopolies. Whether this survival of the fittest in the onward march of civilization must be considered an undisguised blessing for the general public, or not, will not be discussed here.

Texas in 1850, being a new State, sparsely populated and far removed from the civilized part of the United States, had no factories at all. There were no cities in Texas then with more than 5000 inhabitants (Houston, Galveston and San Antonio). The nearest city of any consequence was New Orleans, that could be reached from Texas only by the old San Antonio wagon road or by ship from Galveston, a distance of nearly 400 miles. There were no railroads in Texas before 1860, when the Houston and Texas Central Railroad between Houston and Millican, 80 miles long, was built. Nine-tenths of the population of Texas in 1850 lived on isolated farms or in small settlements, of which New Braunfels, La Grange, Victoria, Fredericksburg, Castroville, Industry, Indianola, Cat Spring and Dhannies were the largest. The pioneer settlers led the most simple life imaginable and even the rich men of the cities did not enjoy any specail comfort or luxuries. Almost everything they used was either homegrown or homemade.

Life on the plantations, cultivated by slave labor, was quite different from that on German farms, or in German settlements. The planter and slave owner with his family generally indulged in a life of ease and indolence, while on the German farms every member of the family worked continuously, often even on Sundays, using in Texas the same intensive system of agriculture as formerly in Germany, in order to clear their land not only of the trees, brush and weeds, but also of the mortgage in the hands of the great land owners, and thus become free and independent farmers in a free country.

Not only in the German settlements, but also in the cities almost all trades and industries were in the hands of thrifty and skilled German mechanics and tradesmen, while the Americans were generally restricted to the vocations of lawyers, physicians, civil engineers, bankers and brokers, land agents, lumbermen, wholesale merchants, cotton factors and public officials. With the German immigrants of the thirties and forties a great many expert workmen and master mechanics had come to Texas, who continued their trade in their new homes as in the Fatherland. But also many of the scientific men and the nobles who had arrived with the colonists of the Adelsverein, often engaged in some industrial or commercial enterprise with more or less success. Robert Kleberg for some time made cigars for the trade, while Dr. Kapp of Sisterdale offered his guests with pardonable pride Havanas grown on his own field and made with his own hands. Count Henkel von Donnersmark and Baron von Nauendorf sold liquor in New

Braunfels, while Baron K. von Zypry dispensed the amber fluid of the New Braunfels brewery. Count von Donnersmark was also the owner of a grocery and hostelry and gained many thousand dollars every year. Dr. Roemer, in his book, "Texas" (1849), says: "Army officers, counts, barons, noblemen, are seen here transformed to ox drivers, teamsters, innkeepers, farmers and servants."

New Braunfels in 1847 had one physician, two drug stores, three bakeries, one brewery, four blacksmith shops, one locksmith, one gunsmith, two beer taverns, six carpenters, five stonemasons, three tanners, one upholsterer, two saddlers, eight cabinetmakers, three wagonmakers and one carriage factory, one brick kiln, a jeweler, several tailors, shoemakers and mechanics of almost every kind. Frederick Law Olmstead, who visited Texas in the early fifties, has the following to say about the German industries at New Braunfels: "I do not think that there is another town in the slave States in which the proportion to the whole population of mechanics or of persons employed in the exercise of their own discretion in productive occupations, is one-quarter as large as in New Braunfels, unless it be some other in which the Germans are the predominating race."

In Galveston, Houston and San Antonio about two-fifths of the population were German in 1850, according to Kapp, while von Behr, writing in 1847, says that Galveston was more than half German; Comal and Gillespie Counties were exclusively German, and Medina and Austin Counties contained more German than American farmers. Nearly all local industries and work shops in the above mentioned cities were conducted by Germans, as were most of the retail stores and establishments. They were all small concerns compared with the stores of today, but sufficient for the wants and needs of that time, and most of the proprietors earned a comfortable living. From them grew many of the largest industrial establishments of Texas, and the foundation of the wealth of many of our rich merchants and professional men was laid 60 and 70 years ago in an insignificant shop, behind which the family lived and toiled in a few small rooms.

The relations between the Germans and the Americans in Texas have not always been as friendly as they are now, or have been for the last 40 years. Before the Civil War there were many sources of disagreements between the two nationalities. Most of the Anglo-Americans in Texas between 1830-1850 had come from Louisiana, Arkansas, Tennessee or other slave States, where there were very few Germans, and the reputation and character of many Americans from the Northern States who had sought new homes in Texas, were not always above reproach, a great number of them being bold and unscrupulous adventurers, while most of the German immigrants were plain, unsophisticated people, striving by hard and conscientious labor to establish new homes for themselves and their families. The American planter and slaveholder firmly believed that manual labor was degrading and looked with derision, mingled with contempt, on the German farmer, plowing his fields and harvesting his crops. This mistaken conception of race superiority was the direct result of the American rule over slaves and continued for some time after the Civil War and after slavery was legally abolished. It is only during the last decades that the sound conviction is growing apace in the minds of all the people that honest labor of any kind should be properly respected, and we are now beginning to realize that we had been victims of the foolish fallacy that manual training is well enough only for those who can not do anything else.

The thousands of German farmers who were continuously and persistently toiling and improving their lands and crops, naturally became formidable competitors of slave labor on the American plantations and increased the lack of harmony between these two different elements of population. The planters became jealous of the German immigrants, while the latter felt that slavery lessened their own value and favored the abolition of slavery from moral reasons.

The German farmers by cultivating their land more judiciously and using intelligent economy, often raised more cotton to an acre than the American planters, and the so-called "free cotton" often brought from 1 to 2 cents more per pound in the markets than that picked by slaves in the same locality. Thus the Germans not only disproved the general belief that cotton could be grown only by slave labor, but also proved that they could grow a superior grade of the staple. All this tended to strain the relations between the Americans and Germans in Texas, and as the latter generally kept closely together in their settlements, they mingled but little with the Americans, except for business purposes, and the opportunity for becoming mutually better acquainted was but scant. Olmstead in his "Journey Through Texas in the Saddle," says: "The manners and ideals of the Texans and the Germans are hopelessly divergent. They make little acquaintance, observing one another, partly with unfeigned curiosity, often tempered with mutual contempt."

Now everything has changed. The Civil War, followed by the abolition of slavery, revolutionized the agricultural system in Texas, the large plantations either being changed into cattle ranches or divided up into small farms, that were either sold or rented to new settlers, and the aristocratic planter gradually disappeared. The Germans were assimilated to American views and ways, and the Americans began to recognize the sterling worth of German immigration. Both nationalities now live and work in perfect harmony in friendly competition for the development of Texas and the continued glory of our great and powerful country.

„Gesang erfreut das Menschenherz
„Uebt wunderbare Kraft
„In Freude, sowie auch im Schmerz
„Er Wonn' und Trost verschafft.

Houston Saengerbund
Houston, Texas

Gegründet ben 6, Oktober 1883.   Organisiert, ben 23, Mai 1884.
Inkorporiert ben 3, Juli 1890.

Chartermitglieder.

Chas. G. Heyne, Paul Dietzschold, Carl Suhm, Chas. A. Dumler, Joe Ressel, Otto Preußner, A. Meister, Gus. Wilkening, Chas. Metzer, Lud. Scharck, A. G. F. Streit, Anton Brunner, William Kummer.

Beamte, 1912-13.

A. Hellberg	Präsident.
W. J. Kohlhauff	Vize Präsident.
A. Brunner	Schatzmeister.
B. Zuenger	Sekretär.

Verwaltungsrat.

L. G. Müller, H. Wolfer, P. Bottler, Wm. Fuchs, P. Ditzschold, A. Kriegel, Joe M. Heiser, Hans Ostrow, H. Albrecht.

Chormeister: C. C. Lieb.

Unser Gruss mit hellem Klang, gilt deutscher Sitte, deutschem Sang!

HISTORICAL SKETCH

OF

TEXAS GERMAN SINGERS' LEAGUE

(STAATS SAENGERBUND)

FROM 1853-1913

BRIEF HISTORY OF THE GERMAN STATE SAENGERBUND OF TEXAS.

For the fourth time in the interesting history of the German State Saengerbund of Texas the City of Houston will be host to the German singing societies that will gather here on May 5th for the celebration of the Twenty-ninth biennial State-Saengerfest. The city is ready to bid a hearty welcome to the German singers and greet them joyfully with:—

"Seid uns willkommen Alle! Gegruesst mit Herz und Hand,
Die Ihr des deutschen Liedes Euch freut in diesem Land!"

The Texas metropolis will entertain the singers royally. Like the Greeks of classical antiquity the Germans are the music-loving nation par excellence of the present time, and the love of song is particularly an innate gift with most of them. The hundreds of folksongs (Volkslieder), the origin of which in many cases cannot be traced, are sung with equal fervor by young and old in the sumptuous palaces of the nobility, as in the humblest cottages of the poor. While the German forests in spring and summer are filled with the joyous warblings of thousands of small singing birds, the highways and fields almost everywhere resound from the merry songs of a lonely wanderer, or the busy toilers of the soil, filling the air with mirth and glee.

The first singing societies (Liedertafeln) in Germany were organized in the beginning of the last century by F. Zelter in Berlin and C. Zoellner in Frankfort-on-the-Main, and their compositions are still among the most favorite songs of the German singers everywhere. Their example worked like an inspiration; it was quickly followed by many teachers of music in North Germany and the beautiful cities along the blessed banks of the Rhine, Neckar and Main

Rivers, and in a few years singing clubs were established in almost every city, large or small, in Western Germany. These singing societies soon became the social centers of the citizens of these towns and fostered a closer union and friendship among them. The first German National Saengerfest was celebrated with the greatest enthusiasm in Frankfort-on-the-Main, on July 28, 29 and 30th, 1838, and 760 singers from various cities between Manheim and Coblenz actively participated in the festival to offer homage at the altar of the fair muse Euterpe. The present membership of all singing societies in Germany is approximately 500,000 and more than 40,000 singers took part in the last National Saengerfest that was celebrated last summer in Nuernberg, Bavaria.

This inherent musical sentiment follows the German wherever he goes, and it may be of some interest to note that the first piano on Texas soil was brought here by Robert Kleberg, Sr., who emigrated to Texas with his family in 1834. This instrument unfortunately became a prey of the flames that destroyed Harrisburg in the spring of 1836, when the hordes of Santa Anna applied the torch to that thriving little town, and many a year passed before the soft strains of a piano were again heard in Texas.

The German immigrants that came to Texas in great numbers from 1845 to 1850 brought along an invisible passenger, "Das deutsche Lied" (the German Song). It accompanied them westward on their dreary march across the broad prairies, where many of the prospective settlers fell by the wayside from exposure and exhaustion, and established itself with the sturdy pioneers on the beautiful banks of the Comal and Piedernales, to cheer them in their daily toil and brighten their evenings at the fireside. Soon some congenial spirits met occasionally under the shady trees on the banks of the silvery Comal at New Braunfels, for the purpose of rehearsing and singing the cherished songs of the Fatherland. On March 2nd, 1850, on the anniversary of the birth of the Republic of Texas, the singing society (Germania), the first singing club in Texas, was organized at New Braunfels. Shortly afterwards German singing clubs were started at Sisterdale, Austin, San Antonio and La Grange, and in the summer of 1853 the "Germania" sent out invitations to these societies to meet at New Braunfels on October 15 for the purpose of celebrating a German Saengerfest.

The First German Saengerfest in Texas.

"Lasst hell erklingen das deutsche Lied
Dass weit es schalle durch Wald und Ried."

The singing societies of San Antonio, Austin and Sisterdale responded to the invitation, that was gladly accepted, and the people of New Braunfels at once began the erection of the first "Saengerhalle" in Texas, on the shady banks of the Gaudeloupe. Although the building was but a rough and primitive structure and the decorations of the simplest, the lack of fineries and modern comfort was amply replaced by the true and unfeigned enthusiasm of all participants, and very likely no subsequent Saengerfest in Texas was celebrated more joyfully and with greater zeal and earnestness than this first festival in New Braunfels. The little burg was all astir, bustle and expectation and young and old vied with each other in preparing a royal welcome to the expected guests. When the day for the opening of the Saengerfest had arrived, it looked as if a superior force would prevent the assembling of the German singers at the young settlement. Diluvial rains that had poured down for more than a week, had changed all the creeks and rivers in West Texas into raging torrents, while the roads were almost impassable. But all these obstacles could not deter the singing societies from fulfilling their promise given to the New Braunfels Club. The singing societies from San Antonio succeeded only with great difficulty in crossing the Salado and Cibolo Creeks, and the Austin singers for a time doubted whether they should risk the crossing of the swollen Blanco River, or not. After long deliberation the attempt was finally made at the risk of their lives, and when they reached the opposite banks they found that nearly all of their effects, including their music books, had been carried away by the waters. All they had saved besides their lives was their banner.

All the singers from San Antonio, Austin and Sisterdale, however, arrived at the proper time, October 15, in New Braunfels, amid the merry cheers of the whole populace, and notwithstanding the fact that the way from the town to the "Saengerhalle" could be made only by wagon, or on horseback, through mire, mud and water, almost everybody in New Braunfels attended the concert of the singing societies on the evening of October 16th. Unbounded enthusiasm prevailed, the Saengerfest became a true Volksfest and the general arrangement committee, consisting of Messrs. G. Eisenlohr, F. Moureau, H. Seele, J. Eggeling and F. Mueller saw with great satisfaction that their untiring efforts were crowned with success.

The following singers participated in the concert that began at six o'clock in the evening, viz.:—

From San Antonio: Fritz Voelkerath, J. Konzen, C. Lane, W. Richter, J. Schmitt, A. Senz, A. Eule, G. Schleicher, F. Enderle, A. Moye, G. Freiselben, Duerler, Lemelson, C. Lege, Elbers, Alex. Strator, J. Conrad, Th. Conrad, Fr. Oswald, J. Riotte and Dr. Adolf Douai, leader.

Sisterdale: Ottomar von Behr, L. von Donop, W. Rhodius, and A. Siemering, leader.

Austin: G. Petmesky, C. Zuschlag, two brothers Pressler, H. Brognaar, Rindel, Aug. Neumann, Wilhelm Schultz, Oppelt, Domsky, Peter Klebar, P. Schmidt, Wm. Kuhfuss, and W. Schmitz; leader unknown.

To these forty singers must be added the "Germania" of New Braunfels, with twenty-four voices, under the leadership of H. Guenther.

German Element in Texas

The following interesting program was ably rendered amid the enthusiastic applause of the whole audience:—

PART 1.

1. Vaterlandslied, A. Marschner, Masschorus.
2. Liebeschmerz, Volksong, Austin Society.
3. Minnelied, J. Otto, Germania Singing Society.
4. Der Tanz, Walz by Otto, San Antonio Society.
5. Das treue deutsche Herz, by J. Otto, Germania.
6. Trinklied, by C. Kreutzer, Sisterdale Quartette.

PART 2.

1. An die Freundschaft, by A. Neithardt, Masschorus.
2. Lebewohl, by F. Silcher, Austin Society.
3. Song of the Spiritis Above the Waters, by Goethe, Sisterdale Quartette.
4. Schlosserlied, by J. Otto, Germania Singing Society.
5. Was ist des Deutschen Vaterland, by Cotta, San Antonio Singing Society.
6. Jaegers Abschied, by Mendelsohn, Masschorus.

After the concert an informal dance was quickly arranged, and although the rain came through the leaky roof in several places, not only the young, but also the older people enjoyed the sport until the early dawn of morning.

During the intermission between the first and second part of the concert, Mr. Hermann Seele, the Mayor of New Braunfels, and the principal of the New Braunfels Academy, delivered the oration, an eloquent panegyric of the German song, and after him Dr. Douay and A. Simering spoke feelingly on the universal liberty of mankind and of the unlimited prospects of the pioneer settlers in the young State of Texas.

After the concert a brief meeting was held, in which a resolution was offered and unanimously passed that another, second Saengerfest, should be celebrated next year in San Antonio.

This second Saengerfest took place on the 14, 15 and 16th of May, 1854, and the singing societies of Austin, La Grange, New Braunfels, Sisterdale and San Antonio participated in the festivities. It would go far beyond the space alloted to this sketch to publish all the programs of the different Saengerfests, and it must suffice to state that the songs rendered at the second and third Saengerfests did not materially differ in style of composition and difficulty of production from those of the first Saengerfest and were all sung a capella.

On March 16, 1854, the last day of the second Saengerfest, according to prearranged plans, a German convention in "Vauxhall Garden" on Alamo Street was held, the program of which had been suggested by the political economists and idealists of Sisterdale, where Ottomar von Behr, A. Siemering and Dr. Kapp were strenuously agitating the principles of social and political freedom and equality, and earnestly advocating the general brotherhood of mankind. Through the eloquence of these men, ably assisted by Dr. Adolf Douay and F. Tielepape, resolutions were adopted demanding the abolishing of capital punishment, the forbidding of speculation in land values, an income and inheritance tax, and declaring slavery a monstrous social wrong that should be abolished in conformity with the Constitution of the United States which declared in emphatic terms that "all men are born free." This resolution also urged non-interference of the United States in the slavery question, but after a State or Territory had abolished slavery, or wished to do so, it should be sustained by the Federal Government.

All these resolutions of the German convention are convincing proof of the radical progressiveness of the German pioneers in Texas, a progressiveness that was far in advance of the times, but somewhat utopian in character. While the participants in the German convention gave an unmistakable proof of the courage of their convictions, their

German Element in Texas 141

public declaration in favor of abolishing slavery in a slave state must be styled an imprudent temerity, as it placed them in direct opposition to the majority of the Americans in Texas, and added materially to increase a feeling of distrust, that the American planters and slave holders held against the German farmers and the Germans generally.

At this second Saengerfest the first steps were also taken for the forming of a German State Singers' League, and a constitution and by-laws, drawn up by a special committee, were recommended to the different societies for adoption.

The third Saengerfest took place at New Braunfels on March 28 and 29, 1855. Of the thirteen invited singing societies the following seven participated: New Braunfels, Indianola, Columbus, La Grange, Austin, Sisterdale and San Antonio. Austin was selected as the meeting place for the fourth Saengerfest in 1856, but the Austin singing society finally declined the honor, and the singers of San Antonio, La Grange and Austin met again at New Braunfels and celebrated the fourth Saengerfest on October 12 and 13th, as guests of the Liedertafel, the second German singing society of New Braunfels. The older society, "Germania," refused to participate in the festivities, and had even announced that on account of the depressed financial condition no Saengerfest would be held. But the Liedertafel was undaunted, and under the energetic management of its leader, H. Guenther, prepared for the fourth Saengerfest, that proved a grand success. The program for the concert contained for the first time a song with musical accompaniment. This was the prize composition "Eine Nacht auf dem Meere" (A Night on the Sea), by A. Tschirch, a difficult chorus work with solos, duetts and orchestra. This latter was replaced by a piano. Mr. Guenther held the baton and Mr. Stademann played the difficult accompaniment with considerable skill. H. Thielepape of San Antonio, W. Schulz of New Braunfels and A. Oppel of Austin, sang the solos and duets of the beautiful composition, which was received with deafening applause by the enthusiastic audience.

In the fifth Saengerfest, which was again held at New Braunfels, only four singing societies, of San Antonio, Austin, and two of New Braunfels, participated. The singing club of Sisterdale had ceased to exist. A delegation from Fredericksburg invited the singers to meet next year at their city. This invitation was gladly accepted and the sixth Saengerfest was celebrated on May 29, 30 and 31, 1859, at Fredericksburg, at that time on the border of civilization, with the following seven societies participating, viz.: New Braunfels "Germania" and "Liedertafel," Fredericksburg, Piedernales, Austin, San Antonio and Grape Creek.

At the seventh Saengerfest at New Braunfels, on March 26, 27, 28 and 29, 1860, the first chorus of mixed voices, the "Concordia" of New Braunfels, rendered two charming songs at the official concert, and many more during the different social gatherings of the Fest. The next Saengerfest had been scheduled for Austin, but early in 1861 the threatening clouds, that had been hanging over the United States for several years, had bursted, the unfortunate and destructive war between the States had begun, and song and music were replaced for years by tears and sorrow.

Several years after the close of the war passed by, before the German societies of West Texas again joined in the celebration of a Saengerfest. On August 22 and 23, 1869, the singers of the two San Antonio clubs, the "Beethoven Maennerchor" and the "Liedertafel," the Austin Society and a club from Boerne, met with the singing societies of New Braunfels at the latter place for the purpose of reviving the German State Singers' League. This was accomplished, a new constitution was prepared and San Antonio chosen for the next, the eighth Saengerfest. This was celebrated on the 9, 10 and 11th of September, 1870, more than ten years after the seventh Saengerfest had been held at New Braunfels. With this Saengerfest an enthusiastic celebration of the great victories of the German armies in France was connected, and the echo of the stirring times that created a German nation and the rejuvenated German empire reverberated in the hearts of the thousands of participants. The ravens no longer flew around Kyffhaeuser mountain, the ban was broken, the barriers between the many principalities were lowered, the marked distinctions between North and South Germany were effaced, and every German felt justly proud of being a son of the Fatherland, of a United Germany. This Saengerfest was by far the greatest that so far had been held. The following cities and towns were represented: New Braunfels (Maennerchor and Liedertafel), Boerne, Comfort, Yorktown, La Grange, and San Antonio. Hopes had been entertained that Houston and Galveston would be represented by singing clubs, or at least by some delegates of such clubs, but no word or representative came from either of these cities, and for several years more participation in the Saengerfests was confined to societies west of the Colorado River. At the business meeting (Tagsatzung) a resolution was adopted to celebrate the Saengerfests henceforth only biennially, and consequently the ninth Saengerfest was held at New Braunfels on May 11, 12 and 13, 1872, in which the following singing societies actively participated, viz.: New Braunfels, Hortontown, Smithsons Valley, San Antonio, Austin, Comfort, Boerne, and the two singing clubs of New Braunfels. In order to perpetuate the love of song in the growing generation and interest them in the forming of new singing societies or joining the existing clubs, the "Tagsatzung" unanimously adopted a resolution that recommended the establishing of singing-schools for children, and for many years such schools were conducted in many cities and towns of South Texas. Not only children of German birth, but also of American parentage were received and instructed in the beautiful art of singing, and the missionary work done by the pupils of these schools ought not to be underestimated. It awakened and fostered among the Americans of Texas the love of music and song, the active agents of a refined life, and the founding of most American singing societies in Texas, as elsewhere, must primarily be attributed to the wholesome influence of these unpretentious singing schools, organized at the suggestion of the German Texas Singers' League.

The tenth Saengerfest was again celebrated in San Antonio in May, 1874, with societies from New Braunfels, Boerne, Comfort, Austin, and Fredericksburg, participating. At this meeting Messrs. A. Groos, H. Bosshard and A. Siemering were appointed as an executive committee to act in the interest of the State Singers' League and prepare a new constitution to be presented at the next Saengerfest. New Braunfels was designated as the meeting place for this Saengerfest, as neither Austin nor any other city represented at the Tagsatzung were willing to be sponsor and host for the next celebration. The attendance of active singers participating in the concerts had constantly grown, and the boarding and entertaining of nearly two hundred participants for three days, with the additional expense for the proper arrangements and other incidentals, amounted to too great a sum, that smaller places would attempt to invite the Saengerfest within their walls. Even New Braunfels, the birthplace of the German Texas Saengerfests, could not raise funds enough for the next Fest and was unable to meet its obligation in 1876, and the executive committee therefore had to find another Verein, willing to undertake the arrangements for the next Saengerfest. The Beethoven-Maennerchor of San Antonio readily accepted the responsibility, and under its auspices the eleventh Saengerfest was celebrated at the Alamo City on the 12th, 13th and 14th of September, 1877.

Eleventh Saengerfest at San Antonio, 1877.

This Saengerfest exceeded its predecessors in many ways. "Fest Praesident" F. Groos, with his chief assistants, A. Siemering, C. Mueller, B. Wolfram, and musical director, E. Zawadil, were equal to their arduous task, and all arrangements were perfect. A new Saengerhall, with a capacity of 1500 seats, had been erected in Central Garden, and an orchestra of 34 pieces for string music had been organized by the indefatigable efforts of Mr. Zawadil, and proved the "piece de resistance" of the whole Saengerfest. The following thirteen singing societies were represented, viz.: Beethoven Maennerchor, Teutonia and Mendelsohn Clubs of mixed voices, of San Antonio, Echo of Smithsons Valley, Austin Saengerrunde, New Braunfels Maennerchor, Boerne Gesang Verein, Liedertafel of Comfort, the singing societies of Yorktown, La Grange, Brenham, and the Galveston Saengerbund. This was the first Saengerfest in which societies from east of the Colorado River participated. The concert, on the second day of the celebration, was a great success from beginning to end, and musical director Zawadil, at the close of it, received an enthusiastic but well deserved ovation for his tireless efforts and his marked ability as an orchestra and chorus leader. The string orchestra opened the concert with the overture from Balfe's melodious opera, "The Bohemian Girl," and later played the overtures from "Martha" by Flotow, and "Nebuchadnezzar" by Verdi. It also played the discreet accompaniment to the Chorus-song, "Meeresstille" by Fischer, rendered with great precision by the Beethoven-Maennerchor, and to parts of Rossini's great composition "Stabat Mater," sung by the Mendelsohn mixed chorus, with Miss Lacoste, Mrs. Karber and Messrs. C. Mueller and A. Karber as soloists. When the sound of the last note of this classical work had ebbed away, there was a grave-like silence for a few seconds, but then an applause broke forth from all parts of the great hall that was filled to overflow, as never had been heard at any previous Saengerfest. The introduction of an orchestra and the singing of chorus songs with orchestra accompaniment had proved so successful that the orchestra from now on became an integral and indispensable part of all succeeding Saengerfests, greatly increasing the budget of these affairs, as every city vied to outdo the other by furnishing a larger and better orchestra. Soon local orchestras and local talent alone did not suffice and soloists as well as whole orchestras were engaged from Cincinnati, St. Louis and Chicago, to add splendor to the concerts and tax heavily the progressive and public-spirited citizens of the cities in which the Saengerfests were celebrated. It was considered impossible to have a Saengerfest without a grand orchestra and some soloists of national fame, and thus the character of the Saengerfests was entirely changed. It is true that the Saengerfests of the last fifteen years have become more metropolitan in style and quality, but it must nevertheless be regretted that now the orchestra and the soloists are the chief attractions of the concerts, instead of the singers. The Saengerfests are unquestionably tending more and more to become great music festivals, with the singing of chorus songs as a necessary adjunct.

At the Tagsatzung the new constitution prepared by A. Groos, F. Bosshard and A. Siemering was adopted with a few changes, and remained in force until 1906, when it was again changed to conform with the changed conditions. During the festivities a number of delegates from the Turnvereins of San Antonio, Houston, New Braunfels, Fredericksburg, West Mill Creek and Quihi, met and organized the "Texas State Turnerbund," adopted a constitution and appointed Houston as "Vorort," with the general offices and next meeting place, and consequently the first State Turnfest was celebrated in Houston in the spring of 1878, in which all associated societies of the State participated.

Austin was selected as the place for the twelfth Saengerfest, and there, in April, 1879, the silver jubilee of the German Texan State's Singers' League was celebrated with appropriate festivities. A virulent yellow fever epidemic ravaging Texas in 1878, had prevented the celebration in that year, as originally proposed, but in order to remember the twenty-fifth anniversary of the Texas Saengerbund in an appropriate manner at the proper time, the Beethoven Maennerchor of San Antonio and the Singing Society from Comfort met with the singers of New Braunfels on October 12th, 1878, at the birthplace of the Saengerbund and celebrated a joyous jubilee meeting on the banks of the silvery Comal.

At the Saengerfest at Austin, the societies of New Braunfels and Comfort were represented for the last time. They did not remain members of the League any longer, but, together with other singing societies of West Texas, formed their own association, the "Gebirgs Saengerbund," which is still flourishing and celebrating its annual Saengerfests in the picturesque cities of West Texas with great enthusiasm, original simplicity and real German "Gemuetlichkeit" (good fellowship).

The Jubilee Saengerfest at Austin, 1879.

Elaborate preparations had been made by the Germans of the Capital City for the proper and dignified celebration of the twelfth Saengerfest, the jubilee of the twenty-fifth anniversary of the State Saengerbund. The Central Committee under the able leadership of Dr. Weisselberg, fest president, and Walter Tips, musical director, ably assisted by Messrs. Ed Schuetze, Samostz, Brueggerhoff, Frischmeier, Stakemann and others, had perfected all arrangements with great skill, finding ready assistance from all merchants and the general public of Austin, and when, on the morning of the 16th of April the singers held their triumphal entry into the city, under the booming of cannon,

Congress Avenue, from the Colorado River to the Capitol, was gaily and profusely decorated with flags and bunting, while two immense arches of honor had been erected, one at the foot of Congress Avenue, the other at the Opera House, where the official concert was held. As a special attraction, the orchestra of the National Theatre of New Orleans, a well known musical organization from St. Louis, had been engaged. The following singing societies participated in the festivities: Beethoven Maennerchor, San Antonio; Maennerchor, New Braunfels; Frohsinn, Dallas; Germania, Brenham; Salamander, Galveston; Saengerrunde and "Gemischter Chor," Austin, and two delegates each from Houston, Comfort and LaGrange. This was the first participation of the societies from Dallas and Brenham at the Saengerfests, while the presence of two delegates from the Houston Maennerchor indicated that the German singers of the Magnolia City would participate at the next Saengerfest. The singers from Dallas, Brenham and Galveston had arrived by a special train in the morning, while the societies of San Antonio and New Braunfels had come overland in sixteen wagons, being received by the entire festival committee, three miles south of the city, in gala coaches and accompanied to the city. At the Colorado River bridge the other singing societies had assembled, and after the arrival of the contingent from New Braunfels and San Antonio, the line of march was quickly formed, the banners unfolded, and the festival march (Festmarsch) to the Opera House begun, cheered all the way by the thousands that lined both sides of Congress Avenue. In the spacious, profusely decorated hall of the Opera House, tables, laden with substantial delicacies, invited the singers to a bounteous repast, and after hunger and thirst had been allayed, Dr. Weisselberg welcomed the singing societies in some well chosen words, to which Mr. H. Seele, of New Braunfels, the nestor of the Saengerbund, responded. Then Colonel De Gress, Mayor of Austin, bade the singers a hearty welcome in the name of the city, handing the freedom and the keys of Austin to them during the Saengerfest. The official oratory closed with some humorous remarks by Mr. Samostz, chairman of the lodging committee, and after the singing of a few impromptu songs, and the faultless rendering of some classical compositions by the orchestra, the joyous assembly adjourned at midnight for a well earned rest after a pleasant but strenuous first day of the jubilee festivities.

The morning of the second day was spent in a general rehearsal of the chorus songs, and in the afternoon an excursion was made to Mount Bonnell, where some pleasant hours were enjoyed. The great concert began precisely at eight o'clock, before a brilliant audience that filled every available seat in the Opera House. The following interesting program was executed with considerable skill:—

PART 1.

Overture Egmont, by Beethoven, Orchestra.
Lob des Gesanges, by L. Maurer, Mass-Chorus.
Zauber der Liebe, by J. Herbert, Salamander, Galveston.
Das Deutsche Lied, by P. E. Schneider, Mass-Chorus and
    Orchestra.
Das Einsame Roeslein, by Hermes, Germania, Brenham.
Phantassie, Die Zigeunerin, by Balfe, Orchestra.

PART 2.

Siegesfeier, by Rheinlaender, Mass-Chorus.
Chor aus Ernani, by Verdi, Mixed Chorus, Austin.
Potpouri, Aida, by Verdi, Orchestra.
Wie hab ich sie geliebt, by Moehring, Frohsinn, Dallas.
Schaeferlied, by Eckert, Mass-Chorus.

PART 3.

Leichte Cavallerie, by Suppe, Orchestra.
Muttersprache, by C. Kuntze, Beethoven, San Antonio.
Bundeslied, by F. Lachner, Mass-Chorus and Orchestra.

Song, by New Braunfels Mannerchor.

Fackeltanz, No. 3, by Meyerbeer, Orchestra.

The orchestra numbers and the mass-choruses, the latter under the firm and effective leadership of Mr. Walter Tips, found especial favor with the attentive and critical audience and were loudly and enthusiastically applauded. A social gathering of the singers at Frischmeires' Hall after the concert pleasantly concluded the second day of the Saengerfest.

On the third and last day the delegates of the societies belonging to the State organization assembled in the forenoon at ten o'clock at Scholz's Garden for the biennial "Tagsatzung." As officers for the next two years Messrs. Walter Tips, president, W. Brueggerhoff, treasurer, and A. Stakeman, secretary, were unanimously elected, and an invitation from Galveston to celebrate the next Saengerfest, the thirteenth, on the sun-kissed shores of the Gulf of Mexico, was received and adopted amid the rousing cheers of all delegates present.

For the afternoon a picnic at Pressler's Garden had been arranged, which was attended by thousands who were carried there by special excursion trains of the I. & G. N. railroad. When Hon. A. W. Terrell, of Austin, mounted the speaker's stand at about four o'clock, the large grounds were filled by an immense multitude of merry and joyous people. In an half hour's speech Mr. Terrell spoke interestingly on music and song, laying particular stress on the debt of gratitude the American people owed to Germany for the introduction of these refining and ennobling arts that brought good cheer and sunshine even into the humblest home. He then paid a glowing tribute to the Saengerfest and German social gatherings generally, which were always so delightful, harmonious and orderly, that they could well form an example and pattern for American entertainments.

After Mr. Terrell had finished amid loud and appreciative applause, Dr. Hadra, of San Antonio, delivered the German oration. It is doubtful whether an equally scholarly German speech has ever been delivered from a Texas rostrum as that of Dr. Hadra at the Saengerfest at Austin in 1879. In a masterful manner and diction on the different problems agitating the minds of the people, he depicted the longing desire in the hearts of many men for intellectual advancement and the materialistic tendencies of the present age. As a softening agent in the turmoil of daily life and strife, he eloquently lauded the music, and among the beautiful art of song, the folklore songs, the "Volksgesang," the real music of the people, of the masses, that captivates mind and soul with its sweet melodies and easy strains. Dr. Hadra concluded his interesting and highly instructive speech with the wish that at the next Saengerfest some American singing society might actively participate as a competitor for the laurels of Apollo, stating that this would be considered the proudest conquest of German pioneer-work in Texas.

A brilliant ball at the Opera House was a fitting finale of the jubilee Saengerfest, that had been of unparalleled success from beginning to end.

Thirteenth Saengerfest at Galveston, 1881.

On May 18th, 1881, the Texas Saengerbund assembled at the fair Oleander City for the celebration of the thirteenth State Saengerfest. The people of Galveston had made extended preparation for this occasion. An immense pavilion with a seating capacity of 5800 had been built at the beach, and there the two concerts of the Saengerfest were held, while the great assembly that filled the spacious hall, was fanned by the cooling breezes from the Gulf. Houston was represented for the first time in the history of the Saengerfests by the Houston Maennerchor, a triple quartette under the direction of Prof. G. Duvernoy, and the following voices: First tenors, O. F. Kuehn, A. Boccius,

A. Baldry; Second tenors, Ernst F. Schmidt, Jacob Binz, E. Raphael; First bassos, Louis Harde, E. Blaffer, Louis Peine; Second bassos, John Reichman, Gus Tips, Jacob Voorsaenger.

The program was the most elaborate of any Saengerfest, containing not only the innovation of *two* great concerts, but being extended over five days instead of three, as had been customary heretofore.

First Day: Reception of singers at 8 P. M. at the Union Depot. Torchlight procession to Artillerie Hall and addresses of welcome by the mayor and chairman of the reception committee.

Second Day: General rehearsal in the morning and afternoon, and first concert at night at 8 o'clock.

Third Day: Rehearsals in the morning, oyster roast and fish chowder on the beach at noon and afternoon; second grand concert at night, followed by a grand ball at the Garten Verein.

Fourth Day: Procession (Festmarsch) of all singing societies, fire department and military companies. In the afternoon, picnic and concert by orchestra in Schmidt's garden, and summernight's festival at night.

Fifth Day: Excursion over the waters of the bay of Galveston and the Gulf of Mexico. Biennial session of delegates of the Texas Saengerbund. Reception and promenade concert in the afternoon at the Garden Verein. At night grand Saenger-Commers (banquet). This extensive program was carried out without the least hitch or impediment. The singers enjoyed the fest immensely and all returned home after having spent five days most pleasantly and agreeably, unanimous in their unlimited praise of the hospitality of the inhabitants of the Island City.

The fourteenth Saengerfest was held in May, 1883, in Dallas. This was the first time the singers of South Texas had gone to North Texas to proclaim the reign of the merry muses of song and music, and great and most favorable was the impression made upon the American citizens of Dallas, many of whom had never before heard a mass-chorus of more than two hundred trained voices. At the Tagsatzung the delegates unanimously passed a resolution that the Saengerfests of the Texas Saengerbund should henceforth be held alternately in Houston, San Antonio, Austin, Galveston and Dallas, and thus the next fest was celebrated in Houston.

This rotation has been kept up regularly since then, only the time having been changed twice to conform with local conditions.

The Fifteenth Saengerfest at Houston, 1885.

Shortly after the Dallas Saengerfest the Houston Singing Society "Maennerchor" ceased to exist, and instead two clubs, the "Liederkranz," Prof. G. Duvernoy, leader, and the "Saengerbund," Prof. C. E. Zeuss, leader, were formed. These two societies, although being active rivals in different matters, worked harmoniously for the success of the coming Saengerfest, the musical arrangement of which was placed in the trusted hands of Professor Duvernoy, while Messrs. Zeuss and Juenger effectively superintended the preparations for changing the large public hall in the market house into an artistically decorated "Saengerhalle." The other necessary arrangements lay in the hands of Mr. John Reichman, President, G. Tips, I. Japhet, L. Harde, L. Kosse, C. Schwarz, E. Raphael, A. Moser and E. Blaffer.

When the opening day of the Saengerfest arrived everything was spick an span. The city was gaily decorated along all the principal streets, Main and Preston, Congress and Travis Streets, however, wearing the most gorgeous apparel. The public spirited merchants along these thoroughfares seemed determined to outdo each other in promoting the spirit of the occasion, and had draped their house fronts in the gayest attire.

The following singing societies took part in this Saengerfest: Salamander and Mendelsohn Societies from Galveston, director, H. Wilkens; Beethoven and Mendelsohn Societies of San Antonio, director, C. Beck; Maennerchor from Austin, director, Walter Tips; Frohsinn from Dallas, director, Chas. Manner; vocal section of Giddings Turnverein, director, A. Krueger; Liederkranz of Victoria, director, H. E. Pursch, and the two Houston Singing Societies, Liederkranz, director G. Duvernoy, and Saengerbund, director, G. C. Zeuss. A chorus of mixed voices was also organized that sang in two of the concerts.

To the official musical program a matinee concert was added by the music committee and this proved so successful that henceforth all Saengerfests offered three concerts to the music loving people of Texas. This addition of a third concert was necessary, as the Saengerbund constantly received new additions to its membership, having now twenty-two singing societies enrolled on its roster. The three concerts of the fifteenth Saengerfest were given before crowded houses on April 28th and 29th, followed on Thursday, April 30th, by a Volksfest at Volksfest Park, and on Friday, May 1st, by a Military Day, with a promenade concert and competing infantry drills, in which companies from Galveston, Brenham and Austin participated. This amusement and entertainment was provided free of charge for everybody and the Saengerfest proved a gratifying success throughout. Prof. Duvernoy the "Festdirigent" was presented by the Saengerfest directorate with a fine gold watch in proper recognition of his valuable and efficient services, while Messrs. Zeuss and Juenger also received official recognition for their artistic work in decorating Municipal Hall.

The sixteenth Saengerfest was held at San Antonio in April, 1887, the seventeenth at Austin in 1889, and the eighteenth at Galveston in April, 1891. In 1890 the Galveston Salamander singing society and the delegations of singing clubs of Houston and San Antonio had gone to New Orleans to participate in the Saengerfest of the North American Saengerbund, that was celebrated at the Crescent City, which visit was returned in 1891 by the New Orleans Quartette Club, under the leadership of Professor Hanno Deiler. The Texas Saengerbund then thought a union of the Louisiana singing societies with the Texas organization probable, but the project did not progress beyond the above mentioned two visits. The New Orleans Society, an old and honored member of the North American Saengerbund, did not wish to sever its connection with this organization, and thus the idea of forming a greater Southern German Singers' League was dropped. This is not to be deplored. The Texas State organization of German singers is strong enough in itself and would lose much of its originality if joined with singing societies of other states.

The nineteenth Saengerfest was held in May, 1893, at Dallas, and the twentieth on May 8th, 9th and 10th, 1894, at Houston.

The Twentieth Saengerfest at Houston, 1894.

The arrangements for the twentieth Saengerfest were intrusted to a general committee made up of delegates of all German lodges and societies and two representatives of the city council, Messrs. Jules Hirsch and John Lyons. Captain F. A. Reichardt was elected President, Moritz Tiling, General Secretary, and M. Kattmann, Treasurer, while to Mr. A. Moser was entrusted the arduous task of raising the necessary funds to defray the expenses of the festival. Nineteen German and three American societies participated in the concerts. These latter were the Musical Union, a mixed chorus of Austin, the Quartette Society of Galveston, and the Houston Quartette Club. Professor Oscar Felden, director of the Houston Saengerbund, was elected musical director of the Saengerfest and Frank Herb, director of the orchestra. As soloists, Miss Clara Landsberg and Mrs.

Bella McLeod-Smith of Houston, Miss Marguerite Fischer of Brenham, Mr. G. P. Warner of Austin, Mr. C. H. Mueller of San Antonio and Mr. W. H. Kirkland of Houston divided applause and honors among themselves. On Thursday, the third day of the Saengerfest, a Volksfest, in Volksfest Park, was arranged, preceded by a grand parade of civic and military organizations through the principal streets of the city.

At several of the preceding Saengerfests soloists and orchestras from Northern cities were engaged, but the directorate of the twentieth Saengerfest had decided, and very properly decided, that in a Texas Saengerfest, Texas musicians and Texas soloists should be engaged exclusively, and consequently only Texas musicians played in the orchestra and home talent sang the solos and sang them well and with artistic finish. Times and conditions of course have changed since then and the arrangements for a Saengerfest now require a much more complicated musical apparatus than twenty-one years ago. With the requirements of greater orchestras and eminent soloists, the budget has materially increased, and while the total expenses for the Saengerfest in 1894 were less than two thousand dollars, the estimated cost of this year's Saengerfest is eight thousand five hundred dollars.

The twenty-first Saengerfest was held in April, 1896, in San Antonio, the twenty-second at Galveston in May, 1898, the twenty-third at Austin in May, 1900, where Mr. G. F. Sauter was elected chairman of the executive committee (Bundespraesident), and the next in Houston in May, 1902.

The Twenty-fourth Saengerfest at Houston, 1902.

The year 1902 did not begin very auspiciously for a festival, the arrangements of which required the procuring of a fund of several thousand dollars, which had to be furnished by a comparative small number of public spirited and broad minded merchants and citizens. The entire country had just passed through a long and severe financial and industrial crisis that had deeply affected all branches of trade and commerce.

Money was very scarce and the duty of the finance committee was far from being a pleasant one. But the Saengerfest had to be celebrated and the necessary fund to be raised. The directors of the Saengerfest were fortunate enough to interest Messrs. H. B. Rice, B. F. Bonner and Captain F. A. Reichardt in the matter and these gentlemen proved to be a very able and efficient finance committee. The officers of the Fest were Dr. K. N. Miller, President, Wm. A. Reichardt, First Vice-President, Dr. H. A. Engelhardt, Second Vice-President, F. Wallrab, Recording Secretary, Wm. Freckmann, Corresponding Secretary, and Maurice Kattmann, Treasurer. These officers were ably assisted by Messrs. J. H. Lilienthal, V. Juenger, Ernst Baumann, L. E. Christiansen, and Wm. Olschewske, who acted as chairmen of the different sub-committees, while Mr. C. C. Lieb was elected director of the mass-choruses (Festdirigent) and Professor E. Lindenberg director of the orchestra. Only two concerts were given at the Auditorium, the matinee concert having been dispensed with, and as an innovation several of the mass-choruses were directed by the leaders (Ehrendirigenten) of different participating singing societies. The soloists of the Saengerfest were Miss Carrie Bridewell, contralto, from the Metropolitan Opera House, New York, and Miss Irma Lieb, pianist, who played with marked ability the difficult "Capriccio Brilliante" Op. 22, by Mendelsohn, with string quintette accompaniment.

The three singing societies of San Antonio, the Beethoven Maennerchor, Deutscher Maennerchor and Liederkranz, and the Frohsinn from Dallas were the first societies to arrive, coming on Sunday evening, and being followed on Monday morning by the singing clubs from Austin, Taylor, Brenham, La Grange, Bellville and Galveston. They were all met at the different railroad depots by members of the reception committee with brass bands and escorted to Turner Hall, where on Monday night the Saengerfest was officially opened by a banquet with following concert, during which the different singing societies sang their choicest solo songs.

The next four Saengerfests were held in Dallas (1904), San Antonio (1906), Galveston (1908), Austin (1911),

Twenty-ninth Saengerfest at Houston, 1913.

This year twenty-one singing societies will meet in Houston for the celebration of the twenty-ninth Saengerfest, at which the diamond jubilee of the State Saengerbund will be fittingly observed. As this year marks the centennial of the great uprising of the German nation against Napoleon's rule and the beginning of the wars of liberation, it would not seem to be amiss if the memory of these stirring times would be also observed in some manner by the coming Saengerfest.

The Texas German Saengerbund can look back with pride on its long career of sixty years, and its missionary work in the field of music and song is universally acknowledged. It will add constantly new recruits to its ranks until it is represented in every city and town throughout the wide domains of our imperial State.

"Herbei zum Kampf des Liedes! Herbei Ihr, Jung und Alt,
Wem immer ward gegeben des Sanges Allgewalt.
Gar eine kraft'ge Waffe, allsiegend ist das Lied.
Es kampft fur Recht und Wahrheit, im Streite nimmer mud.'"

As executive officers (Bundesbeamte) for the period between the twenty-eighth and twenty-ninth Saengerfest, Messrs. A. Hellberg, president, Paul Dietzschold, treasurer, and Vinecnt Juenger, secretary, had been elected at Austin. For the purpose of keeping up a constant interest in the coming Saengerfest, the executive committee published a quarterly magazine (Saenger-Zeitung), which was ably edited by Mr. C. C. Lieb, each number containing much valuable and interesting information for singers and music-loving people generally.

The musical attractions for the twenty-ninth Saengerfest will not only equal, but in some respects surpass, any of the previous celebrations, as the following list will demonstrate:

The St. Louis Symphony Orchestra, 55 men, under the leadership of Max Zach.

Mme. Marie Rappold, prima donna soprano of the Metropolitan Opera Company of New York.

Carl Schlegel, baritone, of Berlin and New York.

Twenty-one German male singing societies, choruses of various Texas cities.

Combined chorus of the Choral Club, the Treble Clef Club and the Quartette Club of Houston, under the joint leadership of Hu T. Huffmaster and Julien Paul Blitz.

Three hundred Houston school children in German chorus and 5000 of them in "America" (matinee only).

The selections of the mass-choruses made by Mr. C. C. Lieb are almost exclusively songs by American composers, two of whom are citizens of Texas—Dr. Hans Harthan of Austin, Texas, and Prof. Frank Renard of Sherman, Texas. The others are Carl Fique, Richard Vossley, Max Muehlert, Dr. Elsenheimer, Carl Kapp, P. Engelskirchen, E. Kempermann, J. Schmidt, A. Buechse, Dr. Felix Jaeger, Theodore Hemberger, J. Mendelsohn, E. Reyl, Otto Wick, Louis Koemmenich, David Melamet and Arthur Claassen. The latter will also lead the chorus songs of the 21 German societies participating in the concerts, the Festhehörde having been fortunate to engage his services for this purpose. Arthur Claassen of Brooklyn, N. Y., is a musician of international fame and unparalleled reputation as a director of singing societies. Thus the musical success of the coming celebration is a foregone conclusion.

HISTORICAL SKETCH

OF

THE HOUSTON TURNVEREIN

FROM 1854-1913

HISTORY OF HOUSTON TURNVEREIN FROM 1854-1913.

In the field of education America owes the kindergarten and manual training to Germany, in social life the singing societies and turner organizations, the progenitors of our athletic clubs.

The former have brightened and enlivened the glumness of the schoolroom, the latter have infused bright cheer, congeniality and good fellowship into men, while also largely contributing to a healthy development of the body.

Among all the clubs and social organizations in our great State, the Houston Turnverein is the only society with the proud distinction of having existed uninteruptedly for nearly three score of years. In Houston the Turnverein has always occupied a prominent position and leading part in the social life of the Magnolia City. Having been organized on the lofty principles of patriotism, physical and mental development and good fellowship, the Houston Turnverein by having unalterably adhered to these fundamental rules, has steadily marched forward and upward until today, and can look back with pride on a continuous career of untarnished honor and well deserved success.

The Houston Turnverein was organized on Sunday, January 14, 1854. In the forenoon of that day there assembled in the house of Mr. Peter Gabel on Preston Avenue, between San Jacinto and Caroline Streets, ten young Germans, true sons of their native country, yet loyal to the principles of American freedom, for the purpose of forming a society, the main object of which should be the physical and mental training of its members, as well as the advancement of social and literary entertainments for their friends.

The original articles of agreement between the members

organizing the Verein with their signatures to the same, are as follows:—

"We, the undersigned, met this day for the purpose of organizing a Turnverein for the practice of brotherly love and the promotion of physical and mental exercises and studies. With this view before us, we have founded the Houston Turnverein under the solemn promise to labor with never failing energy and persistency for its welfare and prosperity.

(Signed)
"W. F. Heitmann,
"Robert Voigt,
"F. Reimann,
"E. B. H. Schneider,
"E. Marschall,
"A. Sabbath,
"Louis Pless,
"E. Schuerer,
"J. Thorade,
"L. Schreihagen.

"Houston, Texas, January 14, 1854."

As the general platform of the Turnverein, the following was adopted, viz.:—

"This society indorses those ideas and principles that originate from a natural and consequently only correct view of life, and therefore, oppose any usurpation of rights and privileges that are not in accord with true liberal principles."

Thus the birth of the Houston Turnverein was effected and announced to the public. All of its founders are now gone to the far beyond, the last one to leave us having been the old, but still young, Captain E. B. H. Schneider, who died in 1903, and who, although 73 years of age, stood to his post as physical instructor of the Turnverein up to a few months prior to his death. In recognition of his long and efficient services, the Turnverein honored the deceased

German Element in Texas

by an official funeral from the hall, where his body lay in state for one day.

The newly organized Turnverein at once took steps to become a factor in the public life of the city. Its members formed at once the first volunteer fire company of the city, and served as such at many fires from 1854 to 1860. The first evidence of their services was at a fire on the 20th of May, 1854, when the Bracken House burned down. In this connection the following note explains itself: Houston, May 21, 1854.—To the Houston Turners: I send you two dozen bottles of ale and porter, which you will please accept as a small token of my appreciation of your services at the fire, and to the city. (Signed) N. Fuller, Mayor.

The membership grew rapidly, being over 50 in 1856, at the end of which year the Turnverein bought its first piece of property, a lot on Caroline Street, between Prairie and Texas Avenues, parts of lots 7 and 8, with a small house on it as an assembly hall. Over half a century has passed since then, but if the shades of the founders of the Turnverein now look down upon the site, where they first installed the happiest club life in Houston, they must rejoice at the gratifying result of their labors and smile benignly on those who now reap so richly of their early sowing.

In 1859 members of the Turnverein organized a military company, known as the Turner Rifles, bought their own uniforms and equipment, and by diligent drill soon became quite efficient soldiers. On several occasions the services of the Turner Rifles were required by the city, and among other duties they guarded for three days the city jail, where in March, 1860, the dangerous desperado and murderer, Kuykendall, was confined. On the night after the Turners had been relieved by a citizens' guard, Kuykendall broke jail and disappeared.

More Property Purchased.

In 1860 the Turnverein bought the two corner lots on

Prairie Avenue and Caroline Streets, adjoining their first bought property, and there built the first Turner Hall, which was dedicated to its use on February 5, 1861, at the seventh anniversary celebration. Dark clouds had at that time risen and threateningly gathered on the political horizon of the United States, and the country was on the verge of the gigantic and disastrous struggle between the North and South, over the principles of State sovereignty and slavery, destined to tear asunder the whole country for four years. If each side had thoroughly understood the other, probably no war would have occurred. But, not understanding each other, "one side," as Lincoln once said, "would make war rather than let the nation survive, and the other would accept war rather than let it perish."

Thus the dedication of the new Turner Hall was celebrated under gloomy forebodings, and the tenseness of the political situation was marked by the draping of the United States flag, which formed part of the decorations, in mourning. In this dedicatory address, Mr. Otto Haun referring to the existing political conditions, and the patriotism of the Turners, spoke the following interesting words:

"Whatever the near future may bring, whenever Texas is going to call her citizens to arms for the protection of the most sacred goods of the people, then the Turners will be among the first to answer that call, and true to their motto, 'Bahn frei' (clear track), will boldly break into the ranks of the enemy."

The Turners as Confederate Soldiers.

A few months later, Texas had joined the secession, the call for volunteers was issued, and the Turnverein raised the first volunteer company in Houston, with E. B. H. Schneider as captain, and most of the officers and men were members of this society. This company was stationed in Galveston and was the first under fire on Texas soil at old South Battery on Galveston Island. When the steamer

Bayou City captured the Harriet Lane in Galveston Harbor, Captain Schneider was dangerously wounded by an accidental explosion of a gun, losing permanently the eyesight of his left eye. The old company flag and an unexploded shell from a Federal man-of-war, are still kept as honored war relics in Turner Hall. In 1862 when Whaul's Texas Legion was organized, the majority of the remaining Turners joined it, and were either elected officers or non-commissioned officers in the following three companies, viz.: O. Nathusius, infantry company, Robert Voigt's company, and H. Wickland's infantry company. These three companies at once joined the Texas Legion, marched to the scene of war and remained in the field until after the surrender of Vicksburg, on July 7, 1863, when they with the other 29,000 prisoners of war were paroled and permitted to return to Texas, the best way they could. They had received their baptism of fire in the battle of Sharpsburg on September 17, 1862, in which Turner Frank Kosse was killed and several others wounded. On January 14, 1863, the members of the Turnverein belonging to these three companies were lying in camp near Grenada, Miss., after General Van Horn's retreat behind the Tallahachie River. All agreed that the anniversary of the Verein should be celebrated, and consequently a general meeting was called in a tent, speeches full of vigor and patriotism delivered, and the ninth anniversary of the Turnverein was there and then celebrated as only Turners and Confederate soldiers in the field could do. Present on this memorable occasion were: O. Nathusius, R. Voigt, L. Wickland, L. Tipendick, H. Behrmann, F. A. Michels, Louis Harde, P. Schwander, C. Warnecke, C. Drescher, J. B. Conrad, G. Loeffler, F. Schurer, Louis Kosse and others. None of the participants of this celebration are any more among us, the last three who departed to the great unknown beyond being F. A. Michels, who died in 1904; Louis Harde, whose death occurred on April 21, 1908, and who was honored by an official funeral from the hall, and Louis Kosse, who answered the call of the grim reaper on August 2, 1910.

Revival of Social Life at Turner Hall After the War.

After the Turner companies had returned to Texas and disbanded, Turner Hall, sadly neglected during the long absence of most of the members of the Verein, was again made cozy and comfortable by willing hands, and the presence of the lively spirits that had created the organization, soon brought back its prominence as a social factor.

In 1866 the Turnverein organized a German-English school, with two competent and able teachers, and an attendance that spoke well for the future of the institution, but in the yellow fever epidemic, which raged in Houston in 1867, the principal of the school, Professor Krittner, died, and his assistant fled from the State. The directors of the Turnverein did not succeed in engaging new and competent teachers for the reopening of the school in the succeeding winter, and thus these unfortunate happenings destroyed the well-meant and otherwise probably successful undertaking, with comparatively great pecuniary loss to the Turnverein.

Under the auspices of the Turnverein, the first Volksfest in Texas was celebrated in 1869 with pronounced success. Mr. Ernest Schmidt was president of the celebration, in which many other German societies from other Texas towns participated. From that time until 1897 the German Volksfest was annually celebrated in Houston, being for years the most prominent public festival in which the population of the entire city, rich and poor, high and humble, equally joined.

On the 18th of March, 1870, the Turners unfortunately lost their hall by fire, but immediately set to work to collect funds for the erection of a new and larger hall, the cornerstone of which was laid with appropriate ceremonies in March, 1871, and which is the hall now used as a ballroom.

The new hall was provided with a large stage, and many an entertaining comedy was played on it by its members, their wives and daughters, who possessed histrionic talent. Messrs. R. Grunewald, E. Leonhardt, J. Bankowski and E. Blaffer were in succession stage directors, and even the rendition of light operas was not too high for their ambition. Before crowded houses and enthusiastic audiences most creditable performances of "Preciosa" and "Tannhaeuser" (parody) were given. A singing society was also formed, which, under the able directorship of Professor G. Duvernoy for many years contributed to the enjoyment and delight of the Turnverein and its friends. This singing society, the "Männerchor," was the first singing society from Houston, participating in a State Saengerfest, in 1885.

On February 24, 1875, some of the younger members of the Turnverein seceded, and together with the sons of some of the older members, started the "Jahn Turnverein," of which Captain Schneider became physical instructor, while Theodore Miller instructed the Turners of the old Verein, but on August 4, 1877, this offspring of the parental root rejoined its older brother, which occasion was duly celebrated with an appropriate concert, summer nights festival and ball. In the same year the "Texanische Turnerbund" was organized at San Antonio, the Houston Turnverein receiving the honor of holding the general offices for the first year. Consequently, the first "Bundes Turnfest" was celebrated in Houston in the spring of 1878, a great festival, in which all the associated societies throughout the State, from Galveston, Brenham, Austin, San Antonio, New Braunfels and Fredericksburg participated.

In June 1877 the Turnverein sustained a great loss in the death of its former president, Mr. Gustave Loeffler, who had presided over the destinies of the Verein for eighteen years and who had been the leading spirit in all German enterprises of Houston for years. For several years Loeffler had also been commissioner of immigration for the State of Texas, and a member of the Twelfth Legislature. His death occurred at San Antonio, whither he had gone in hopes to regain his shattered health, on June 4th; the body was brought to Houston. He was accorded an official burial and at the grave, Mr. Louis Harde held the eulogy, ending with the following impressive words: "He was a true friend to his friends, a brother to the Germans of Texas, a brave champion of their rights, and a combatant of truth. His motto was 'Bahn frei für Wahrheit Licht und Aufklärung' (clear track for truth, enlightening and progress). Let us keep this motto forever sacred."

Charter Secured.

After the new hall had been finished in 1871 the Verein decided to become an incorporated society, and on December 1 of that year the Governor signed the charter of the Houston Turnverein, granted by the Legislature of the State. As incorporators were named: G. Loeffler, F. W. Heitmann, I. Veith, L. Harde, L. Kosse, R. H. Cabanis, J. D. Usener, G. A. Meyer, E. L. Leonhardt, P. R. Westen and F. A. Michels. R. H. Cabanis is now the only survivor of these incorporators.

As the only surviving charter incorporator of the Turnverein and one of its earlier members R. H. Cabanis is an interesting link between the Turnverein's early struggles for existence and its present flourishing condition, that has kept apace with the marvelous growth of Houston. Mr. Cabanis was born in Silberberg, Silesia, on January 27, 1833, moving to Texas with his parents in November, 1846. He joined the Turnverein in January, 1858, and has been a member for 55 years, being in point of age and membership the nestor of the Turnverein, closely followed by Mr. Theodore Miller, who became a member in 1861.

After the incorporation the history of the Turnverein has been one of continued triumphs and success. Political or religious connections were never allowed to intrude upon the freedom of pleasure and social mingling that was the life of the Verein, and while a great many Americans became members, the management of the business affairs of the Turnverein rests entirely in the hands of the active German members.

In the year 1903 the membership of the Turnverein had increased so much that the club rooms and the hall built in 1871 had become entirely too small. In order to meet the pressing demand for larger and more convenient accommodations, the board of directors after long and careful discussions and deliberations, submitted to the members plans for an additional structure to the old hall, and a remodeling of the grounds by removing the bowling alleys to the Prairie Avenue side, at the same time enlarging it. These plans were adopted by a general meeting and the building at a cost of $15,000 erected, thus giving the Turnverein the largest and best equipped hall in the State of Texas.

During the last 10 years the ranks of the old members have been greatly thinned through the grim reaper, Death, and the Turners had to mourn the loss of many of the most energetic and devoted members of the Verein. Among those who left us may be prominently mentioned, August Moser, who died in October, 1898, and who as the long time president was the life and soul of the Turnverein; then Ferdinand Hacker, Louis Meyer, Henry Hartmann and Charles Herrmann, the latter two at the time of their death occupying the office of vice president; Fred Schweikart, Maurice Kattmann, who for 14 years was the faithful and trusted secretary of the Turnverein, and the eight oldest members—John Zimmermann, Captain E. B. H. Schneider, Frank Michels, Dr. Erich Schmidt, Louis Harde, Louis Kosse, J. Danielson, Sr., and Jacob Binz, who departed from us only a few weeks ago.

The Golden Jubilee.

The golden jubilee of the Turnverein was celebrated in

an elaborate manner on Thursday January 14, 1904, in a manner befitting the importance of the event. The arrangement committee of the celebration, of which L. E. Christiansen was chairman, had done everything in the scope of decorations and arrangements to make it a memorable festivity. Many hundreds of bright and expectant faces greeted Dr. Max Urwitz, then president, when he ascended the platform in the large hall to address the Turners at the morning exercises, and at the banquet following, in which the city and county officials participated, many happy toasts congratulatory of the Turnverein were spoken and enthusiastically cheered by the hundreds of participants.

Moritz Tiling had written a festival poem and published a booklet in German and English, containing a brief history of the interesting history of the Turnverein, that was handed to all guests present as a fitting memorial of this important landmark in the life of the Verein. The grand ball on the evening of January 14, that concluded the jubilee festivities, was a gala affair in the full meaning of the term. The large hall in its dazzling decorations of gold and purple, looked gorgeous in the bright light of hundreds of electric globes, and was filled to its capacity with a joyous mass of dancers until the early hours of dawn.

Death of Dr. Urwitz.

On October 2, 1905, the Turnverein sustained a severe loss through the sudden death of its honored and beloved president, Dr. Max Urwitz, who died of apoplexy. In due respect to the character and sterling qualities of the deceased his remains were carried to Turner Hall, where they lay in state and where at 8 p. m. elaborate public funeral services were held. Dr. Henry Barnstein opened the ceremonies with the Jewish service. He was followed by Mr. M. Tiling, who in behalf of the Turnverein, delivered a eulogy in the German language, taking occasion to pay high tribute to the manly virtues represented in Dr. Urwitz's character. Messrs. H. Fischer and A. B. Langermann, two intimate friends of the departed, spoke feelingly in English, while during intervals the Saengerbund and the Elks' Quartette rendered beautiful and impressive mourning songs.

Then, as mentioned above, Louis Harde died on April 21, 1908, and Louis Kosse on August 2, 1910. Of the old members of the sixties of the last century, only Messrs. R. H. Cabanis and Theodore Miller survive, and are still members of the Turnverein.

From the beginning the Turnverein has adhered to the sound policy of acquiring as much property for the Verein as was consistent with strict business principles, and in course of time became the owner of the entire block on which in 1855 the Turners bought their first lot. This policy has proved highly beneficial. The phenomenal increase of property values in Houston's business district during the last five years, and the great demand for such property resulted in many offers made to the Turnverein for the sale of all, or part of the Verein's property. The directors persistently refused all offers, until finally the offer of the Taylor-Guthrie Company for half of the block, fronting on Texas Avenue, from Caroline to Austin Streets, was accepted, and on June 26, 1911, these six lots were sold for the sum of $168,000, the Verein retaining the other half of the block fronting on Prairie Avenue. By this advantageous sale the Turnverein could not only pay the different mortgages on its property, but had enough funds left for a new and substantial hall and club building. A building committee, consisting of Messrs. L. E. Christiansen, chairman; A. Hellberg, S. Taliaferro, L. F. Schweikart and L. F. Dormant was appointed, that finally adopted the plans of Sanguinet, Staats and Barnes for a new hall, which is now in course of construction at the corner of Austin Street and Prairie Avenue. The building, of pressed brick and stone, is four stories high, costing one hundred thousand dollars, while the interior equipment will necessitate a further sum of twenty thousand dollars. The Houston Turnverein will then possess the finest and best equipped clubrooms in the entire South.

The lower floor, which is known as the ground floor, same being practically at grade level, will have in same the bowling alleys, also the Turners' school, the kitchen which will serve the club room floor, shower baths, lockers, toilet rooms, etc., for both Turners and bowlers.

The floor directly above is intended to be used for club room purposes, officers' rooms, etc. There will be on this floor the club room, assembly room, buffet, ladies' parlors, library, also main entrance and lobbies, elevator and two stairways leading up to the ball room and banquet room floor.

The upper floor, which in reality consists of two floors, will comprise the main ball room, the stage, dressing rooms, etc., and will have in addition to this a gallery, or mezzanine floor, which can be used as a gallery in the event that the main hall is used for theatrical or convention purposes. This gallery can also be arranged to be used strictly for banquet purposes, if so desired.

The stage, as designed, has a proscenium opening which is as large as the average opera house throughout the country, and the stage itself will seat between 300 and 400 people thereon, making it very desirable to use for such purposes as conventions, meetings, etc., where a number of speakers are expected to be seated on the platform, or for massed choral effect such as the Saengerfest.

The ball room proper is 70 by 90 feet, without any posts in same, making it the largest ball room in the State with an absolutely clear space.

Present Membership of the Turnverein.

Thus the affairs of the Turnverein are in a highly satisfactory and flourishing condition. The present membership consists of 275 active and 253 passive members, with the following 32 honorary members, who for 25 years and more have uninterruptedly been members of the Verein, on the honor list: Henry Albrecht, S. S. Ashe, James A. Baker, Jr., James Breeding, George R. Bringhurst, Anton Brunner, R. H. Cabanis, William Cameron, W. A. Childress, H. F. Fisher, C. J. Grunewald, F. A. Heitmann, M. Henninger, C. G. Heyne, C. H. Hoenke, V. Juenger, Henry Kasche, R. W. Knox, James Masterson, Theodore E. Miller, C. G. Pillot, H. B. Rice, C. C. Rugers, W. W. Schmidt, H. O. Schneider, J. W. Schneider, L. B. N. Schneider, L. F. Schweikart, Moritz Tiling, Gus H. Tips, H. Waddell, J. A. Ziegler.

The management of the Turnverein is at present confided to the following board of officers and directors: W. W. Schmidt, president; C. H. Kuhlmann, vice president; F. P. Kalb, treasurer; L. F. Schweikart, secretary; who with Messrs. Henry Albrecht, J. C. Goldstein, Hermann Schneider, Gus Dreyling, Henry Kriechhamer, L. E. Christiansen and L. B. Schulte form the board of directors.

We are prevented from looking into and from knowing the future, or even lifting the veil that shrouds coming events from the human eye, but so much may be predicted without any degree of presumption that there is still a long time of social usefulness in store for the Turnverein, and that it will continue to flourish as long as its members adhere strictly to the lofty principles on which the Turnverein was founded, and as long as the management of its business affairs remain in trusty and capable German hands as heretofore.

GERMAN DAY CELEBRATIONS IN HOUSTON.
For Twenty-one Years, 1889-1910.

Firmly established, wherever the German idiom sounds within the wide borders of our great and beautiful country, is German Day. The result of arduous labors of Professor O. Seidensticker, and the late G. Kellner, editor of the Philadelphia Democrat, the first German Day was celebrated in the city of William Penn on October 6, 1883. From there the idea spread rapidly over the whole United States, and today, from the populous shores of the Hudson River to the romantic Golden Gate, and from the dense forests of Wisconsin to the sunny prairies of Texas, German Day is the cherished inheritance of all true and loyal German-American citizens.

German Day shall, primarily, commemorate the landing of the first German Colony on American soil on October 6, 1683, but it shall also remind us of the everlasting, faithful work and the achievements of the German element in the United States in art, literature, education and in all industrial branches. It may safely and without any exaggeration be asserted that the Germans have taken a leading part in the civilization and development of our country, and preeminently so in the great State of Texas, and the celebration of German Day is therefore the proper expression of the just pride and satisfaction the present race feels over works accomplished by our fathers. Hon. Carl Schurz, in a speech delivered at the St. Louis Exposition, said: "German Day in the United States is the celebration of the friendship of the German and the American people. The German-Americans are the hyphen between Germany and America, presenting the living demonstration of the fact that a large population may be transplanted from one to another country, and may be devoted to the new fatherland for life and death, and yet preserve a reverent love for the old."

In Houston the first German Day celebration took place in the year 1889. At a called mass meeting held in Turner Hall the subject of celebrating this day was discussed and it was finally resolved to celebrate German Day on the 6th of October of that year. Mr. August Moser was elected president of the celebration, while Dr. Max Urwitz was appointed orator of the day. Both have since departed to the great Unknown Beyond, but their memory is still fresh and revered by the large circle of their many true and devoted friends. The entire German population of Houston and Harris County took part in the festivities, which were held in Turner Hall, and thus the first celebration of German Day in Houston was ushered in and proved an immense success.

In the years 1890 and 1891, the Turnverein arranged the celebration of German Day, and on both occasions Mr. A. Moser delivered the German address, the text of which was published by the Houston Post in full, in the German language.

The year 1892 witnessed a German Day celebration of extraordinary magnificence. This year being the four hundredth anniversary of the discovery of our Continent, it was deemed proper that the festivities should be arranged on broad and exhaustive plans. The German-American Citizens' Alliance took up the matter and after a great deal of deliberation, decided in favor of a two days celebration. On October 20, the festivities began with a vocal and instrumental concert in the opera house, and the production of historical and allegorical tableaux, in which more than a hundred ladies and gentlemen participated. On the next day, the first great German Day parade moved through the streets of the city of Houston. The parade consisted of four divisions under the command of Grand Marshal Charles Hirzel, and twenty marshals. Eight floats artistically built and decorated by the Messrs. L. Hartmann, V. Juenger and K. Stock, called for the constant applause and unbiased admiration of the thousands of spectators who lined the streets through which the pageant passed. Besides the German associations of Houston all the gun clubs of Harris County and the Uniformed Rank of the Knights of Pythias took part in this parade. For the afternoon a great Volksfest had been arranged in Volksfest park and thousands listened to the orations of Captain J. C. Hutcheson, George B. Griggs, and Moritz Tiling. A dance in Volksfest park and a ball in Turner Hall concluded this memorable celebration.

The German Days of 1893, 1894 and 1895 were held alternately at Turner Hall and at Volksfest park under the auspices of the Houston Turnverein and Houston Saengerbund. The orators at these occasions were the Hon. W. P. Hamblen, Hon. S. H. Brashear, Hon. H. B. Rice, Alexander Earttlingck, A. B. Langermann and Moritz Tiling.

The next prominent German Day celebration took place in the year 1896. The executive officers for this celebration were Moritz Tiling, President; John Steinhagen, Vice-President; A. Brunner, Treasurer; V. Juenger, Secretary; Ben A. Riesner, Chairman of Finance Committee, and Captain F. A. Reichardt, Grand Marshal. The gorgeous street pageant, which ushered in the festivities in the morning, surpassed in brilliancy anything the people of Houston had witnessed in this line before.

The daily press in commenting on the parade, said the following:—

"To President Tiling is certainly due much credit for the brilliant success of yesterday's event. No such parade has before traversed the strets of Houston, and such parades have deteriorated so much of late that the magnificence of yesterday's turnout was a subject of universally favorable comment. The parade rivalled anything of the kind ever given in Houston. It was a handsome pageant and the ideas expressed in the decorations, in the arrangements and in the distributions of characters were excellent and excited the admiration of every one who viewed the line as it passed."

In 1897 the year of the dengue fever, German Day was celebrated in Forest Park, with Mr. Julius Schuetze, Sr., of Austin, orator, and despite the quarantine established in many places around Houston, was quite successful.

In 1898, the year of the Spanish-American war, Mr. F. Hacker was president of the German Day committee. The celebration took place at Turner Hall gardens, the orators of the occasion being Dr. Urwitz and Captain Hutcheson. In deference of a German custom, a young oak tree (Friedenseiche) was planted at the northwest corner of the Turner Hall block and dedicated to the care of the people of Houston. Children's games and exercises, productions of tableaux, arranged by Mr. V. Juenger, and a grand ball were the special features of this celebration.

Next year (1899), German Day was celebrated by the Houston Saengerbund in the new Saengerbund hall with Mr. M. Tiling as orator of the day.

In 1900, German Day was again celebrated on a large scale. The festivities began with a concert in the afternoon at Turner Hall garden, interspersed with songs and exercises of 250 children, under the direction of V. Juenger, and gymnastics by members of the Turnverein under the direction of the late Captain E. B. H. Schneider. The oration was delivered by the Hon W. A. Trenckmann of Bellville, and at night a festival play, "All Hail, Columbia," and tableaux, personifying the developments of gymnastics, were set on the stage, while the usual grand ball finished the day's exercises. The officers of that year's celebration were M. Tiling, President; G. F. Sauter, First Vice-President; F. Wallrab, Second Vice-President; M. Kattmann, Treasurer; and C. C. Lieb, Secretary.

From 1901 to 1907 Mr. G. F. Sauter was president of the German Day general committee, which in June, 1906, was changed into the Houston German Day Association (Inc.). The charter was signed as incorporators by G. F. Sauter, L. Gus Mueller, V. Juenger, C. C. Lieb and L. C. Christiansen, and as directors for the first year, besides these incorporators, were named Dr. H. A. Engelhardt, G. P. Zeiss, M. Tiling, F. H. Potthoff, Wm. A. Reichardt and Wm. Fuchs.

Since the year 1900 to 1908, the yearly German Day celebrations have not differed materially from each other, each being held without much outward display at Turner Hall, and consisting mainly of children's songs and calisthenic exercises, speeches in German and English, vocal and instrumental concerts and concluding with the customary ball.

German Day celebration in 1909 was the first since many years in which the German-American citizens of Houston went prominently before the public, and under the direction of President A. Hellberg and Grand Marshal Wm. Bottler, proved conclusively that the spirit of former years had only been dormant, but not extinct. The splendor of the great street parade, the "clou" of carnival celebration, is still fresh in the memory of all who saw, applauded and admired it, and does not need to be extolled.

Extensive preparations had been made for the celebration in 1910, which exceeded in its scope and the magnificence of its parade any previous festival. The orators on this occasion were Governor-elect O. B. Colquitt, and J. C. von Rosenberg, Grand President of the Order of the Sons of Hermann in Texas. The great pageant was again under the command of Grand Marshal Wm. Bottler, while Messrs. V. Juenger, C. Stock and C. W. Hille, with a strong corps of assistants had for two months been industriously engaged planning, building and decorating twelve gorgeous and artistically finished floats that in beauty of conception and elegance of execution, eclipsed anything heretofore seen in Houston.

WORKS FOR BIBLIOGRAPHICAL REFERENCES.

Aufforderung und Erklärung in Betreff einer Auswanderung im Grossen aus Deutschland in die nordamerikanischen Freistaaten, Giessen, 1833.

Auswanderer nach Texas, der. Ein Handbuch und Rathgeber für die, welche sich in Texas ansiedeln wollen. Bremen, 1846.

Behr von, Ottomar: Guter Rath für Auswanderer nach den Vereinigten Staaten von Nord America mit besonderer Berücksichtigung von Texas, Leipzig, 1847.

G. G. Benjamin: Germans in Texas, Philadelphia, 1910.

Berghaus, Heinrich: Die Vereinigten Staaten von Nord Amerika, Gotha, 1848.

Bromme, Trautgott: Neustes vollständigstes Hand- und Reisebuch für Auswanderer, Bayreuth, 1846.

Bruncken, Ernest: German Political Refugees in America, 1815 to 1860; Chicago, 1904 (reprint of Deutsch-Amerikanische-Geschichts-blätter, 1904).

Buettner, J. G.: Briefe aus und über Amreika, oder Beiträge zu einer richtigen Kenntniss der Vereinigten Staaten von Nord Amerika und ihrer Bewohner; Dresden and Leipzig, 1845.

Douai, Adolf: Land und Leute in Amerika; Berlin, 1864.

Duden, Gottfried: Bericht über eine Reise nach den westlichen Staaten Nordamerikas und einen mehrjährigen Aufenhalt am Missouri in den Jahren, 1824, 1825, 1826, 1827. St. Gallen, 1832.

Ehrenberg, Hermann: Der Freiheitskampf in Texas; Leipzig, 1844.

Ehrenberg, Hermann: Texas und seine Revolution; Leipzig, 1843.

Eickhoff, Anton: In der neuen Heimath (zweite Ausgabe). New York, 1885.

Fest-Ausgabe zum fünfzigjährigen Jubiläum der deutschen Kolonie Friedrichsburg. Eine kurzgefasste Entwickelungs-Geschichte der vom Mainzer Andelsverein gegründeten Kolonien in Texas. Fredericksburg, Texas, 1896, by Robert Penninger.

Grund, F. J.: The Americans. 2 vols. London, 1837.

Hecke, J. Valentin: Reise durch die Vereinigsten Staaten von Nord Amerika in den Jahren 1818-1819. 2 vols. Berlin, 1821.

Hoehne, Friedrich: Wahn und Ueberzeugung. Seine Reise von Weimar über Bremen nach Nordamerika und Texas in den Jahren 1839-1841; Weimar, 1844.

Kapp, Friedrich: Aus und über Amerika, Thatsachen und Erlebnisse. 2 vols. Berlin, 1876.

Kapp, Friederich: Die Geschichte der deutschen Ansiedelungen des westlichen Texas und dessen Bedeutung für die Vereinigten Staaten (in Atlantische Studien, ol. 1, p. 173, ff).

Kapp, Friederich: The History of Texas, Early German Colonization, Princes and Nobles in America, the Future of the State; (in New York Tribune, Jan. 20, 1855).

Loeher, Franz: Geschichte und Zustände der Deutschen in Amerika; Cincinnati und Leipzig, 1847.

Meusebach, John O.: Answers to Interrogatories; Austin, 1894.

Olmsted, Frederick Law: A Journey Through Texas or a Saddle Trip on the Southwestern Frontier (Our Slave States, Vol. II), New York, 1860.

Roemer, Ferdinand: Texas. Mit besonderer Rücksicht auf deutsche Auswanderung und die physischen Verhältnisse des Landes. Bonn, 1849.

Rosenberg, William von: Kritik der Geschichte des Vereins zum Schutze der deutschen Auswanderer nach Texas. Austin, 1894.

Scherpf, G. A.: Entstehungsgeschichte und gegenwärtiger Zustand des neuen unabhängigen amerikanischen Staats Texas. Ein Beitrag zur Geschichte, Statistik und Geographie dieses Jahrhunderts, im Lande selbst gesammelt. Augsburg, 1841.

Sealsfield, Charles (Carl Postl): Life in the New World, or Sketches of American Society. Translated from the German by G. C. Mackey. New York, 1844.

Sealsfield, Charles: The Cabin Book, or Sketches of Life in Texas. Translated from the German by C. H. Mersch. New York, 1844.

Soergel, Alwin H.: Neuste Nachrichten aus Texas; Eisleben, 1847.

Texanische Monatshefte ,L. F. Lafrentz, XIII Vols. San Antonio, 1895-1909.

Wrede, Friederich von: Lebensbilder aus den Vereinigten Staaten von Nord Amerika und Texas. Cassel, 1844.

LANDUNG IN GALVESTON. WEITERFAHRT NACH PORT LAVACA.
am 26. November 1844.
Von Fritz Goldbeck.

Hurrah, hurrah, das Prärieland!
Am Horizont erglänzt der Strand,
So rief's herunter aus den Wanten,
Laut jubelten die Emigranten.
Der Lotse, ein gebräunter Mann,
Kam flugs im Segelboot heran,
Lenkt sicher unser schiff zum Hafen;
Wir konnten einmal ruhig schlafen.
Da waren wir in Galveston!
Wer hätte nicht gehört davon;
Damals war dort nicht viel zu holen,
Heut zählt es zu den Metropolen.
Von Galveston nach kurzer Rast,
Auf kleinem Schiff mit einem Mast,
Fuhren wir nach Port Lavacca weiter,
Der Himmel war bis dahin heiter.
Recht tröstlich klang für uns das Wort:
"Bis morgen Mittag seid ihr dort,
Noch einmal vierundzwanzig Stunden
Und Alles habt ihr überwunden!"
Nicht wie der Mensch es wünscht und denkt
Das Schicksal seine Bahnen lenkt,
Denn in den nächsten schlimmen Tagen
Gabs viel zu jammern und zu klagen.
Gleich in der Nacht der Sturm brach los,
Als käm er aus dem Höllenschoss
Mit Brausen, Aechzen, Heulen, Pfeifen,
Der tollen Windsbraut rasend Keifen.

Der Sturm entführte unser Boot,
Ein Leck im Schiff, es wuchs die Noth,
Voll war damit der Unglückshumpen,
Man griff verzweifelt zu den Pumpen.
Im Schiffsraum sah es traurig aus,
Dort herrschten Schrecken, Angst und Graus,
Zum Tod geängstigt, weinten, klagten,
Die Menschenkinder, die Verzagten.
Oft habe ich zurückgedacht
An jene grauenvolle Nacht,
Die Leut' beim Pumpen festgebunden,
Verlebten schrecklich bange Stunden;
Die Wellen stürzten über Deck
Und Arbeit heischte stets das Leck,
Steif wurden die durchnäszten Kleider,
Denn eisig blies der Norder leider.
Der Sturm trieb uns mit wildem Drang,
Fort, fort, wohl eine Woche lang,
Gen Süden durch die Wasserwüste
An Merikos entfernte Küste.
Zum Glück kam dann von Süd der Wind,
Der führte uns zurück geschwind,
So dasz auch schon in wenig Tagen
Wir an der Texas Küste lagen.
Nacht wars, der Eingang zu der Bai
Sehr seicht, wir legten darum bei;
Der Anker lag in gutem Grunde,
Wir schliefen sanft schon manche Stunde,
Da weckte uns ein jäher Stoss—
Der Satan war schon weider los,
Vom neuen Norder angeblasen
War wiederum das Meer am rasen.
Die starke Ankerette brach,
Die bösen Geister blieben wach,
Um jede Hoffnung zu ermüden,
Trieb unser Schiff nochmals gen Süden.

Ein ander Unheil wurd' bekannt,
Es fehlte bald an Proviant
Und, wenn das Schicksal es nicht wende,
Geh süszes Wasser auch zu Ende.
Zum Heil der Norder, Anfangs schlimm,
Liess nach mit seinem wilden Grimm,
Wir thaten uns auch nicht genieren
Und gingen tapfer an's lavieren.
Das Unglück war wohl endlich müd,
Die Brise legte um nach Süd,
Ein jeder von uns, wieder kregel,
Half ziehen an dem groszen Segel.
So fuhren wir zur Bai hinein
Mit Singen, Iubeln, Iauchzen, Schrein.
Hell glänzten unseres Glückes Sterne,
Lavacca zeigte sich von Ferne!
Mit Tüchern winkte man vom Strand,
Der dichtgedrängt voll Menschen stand,
Man hatte uns schon aufgegeben,
War nun erfreut, dass wir am Leben.

Die Landreise nach der neuen Colonie (später Neu Braunfels.) 1845.

Wir zogen aus Lavacca fort,
Von Lagerort zu Lagerort,
Bedächtig langsam fortgetragen
Auf groszen schweren Ochsenwagen.
Im consequenten Schneckengang
Bewegten wir uns wochenlang
Durch graue wogende Prärien,
Sahn dort das Wild in Rudeln ziehen.
Nicht ohne Reiz war jene Zeit,
Wir hatten oft Gelegenheit
Uns Intressantes anzusehen,
Und kounten immer jagen gehen.

Wild jeder Gattung ohne Zahl,
Der Iäger hatte freie Wahl,
Die Prärie bot ihm reiche Birsche
Es gab dort Hühner, Gäns und Hirsche,
Die Enten und das Wasserhuhn
Bekamen selten Zeit zum ruh'n.
Oft knallte es in allen Ecken,
So dass die Thierwelt muszt erschrecken.
Den weiten Weg herauf vom Golf
Hielt Nacht's Concert der Präriewolf
Bei irgend welchen todten Rindern,
Ganz ungefährlich selbstden Kindern.
Truthähne kollerten im Wald,
Der Wagenführer rief sien Halt,
Dann knatterte ein Rottenfeuer
Und der Erfolg war ungeheuer.
Die Frauen waren drob erstaunt,
Dass so das Iagdglück sei gelaunt;
Wer sah denn je zevor dessgleichen,
Ein halbes Dutzend Puterleichen.
Nur selten traf man eine Farm,
Wenn es geschah, gab es Alarm.
Da wurde viel gestaunt, bewundert,
Die Kühe zählte man beim Hundert,
Und gastlich war jedwedes Haus,
Die Leute kamen gleich heraus,
Erfreut die Hände uns zu drücken,
Mit Speis und Trank uns zu erquicken.
Man brachte Eier, Milch und Brod,
Es herrschte Ueberfluss statt Noth;
Mit Freuden hat man's uns gegeben,
Ein wirklich paradiesisch Leben.
Es hat natürlich nicht verfehlt,
Und uns mit frohem Muth beseelt.
Doch ist's nicht lange so geblieben,
Kam viel zu oft, ward übertrieben.

Iagdabenteuer gab es viel,
Der Spottlust dienten sie als Ziel.
Ein Iäger es gar sehr bereute,
Da er ein Stinkthier bracht als Beute;
Ein Andrer hatte viel Verdruss
Durch seinen wohlgezielten Schuss,
Der Truthahn, der von ihm erlegte,
Die Lachlust allgemein erregte!
Des Vogels Duft, fürwahr kein Spasz,
Stieg ganz bedenklich in die Naf',
Ein Missgriff auf der der alten Leier,
Der Truthahn war ein Buzzard-Geier.
Gleich oberhalb Vivttoria
Sahn wir die ersten Tonqueva,
Die rothen, häszlichen Gesellen,
Bekleidet mit gegerbten Fellen.
Wir wurden auch am Weg bekannt
Mit dem verwünschten Präriebrand,
Und konnten, um ihm auszuweichen,
Noch grad den Uferwald erreichen.
An Pferden hatte jeder Freud,
Die groszen, wie die kleinen Leut,
Manch einer ritt da, stolz im Glücke,
Bis ihn ereilte Schicksalstücke,
Sein spanisch Ross es hielt sür Pflicht,
Und bracht ihn aus dem Gleichgewicht.
Der Aermste lag alsdann im Grase
Und rieb sich die geschund'ne Nase.
Dann kamen wir zur Guadalup,
Der Fluss, wie ein recht böser Bub,
War unmanierlich, stark am Tollen,
Recht überflüssig angeschwollen.
Wie nach der Schrift es einst geschah,
So saszen auch wir trauernd da
Und schauten auf den Strom, den trüben,
Die neue Heimath lag ja drüben.

Am Tag darauf, noch früh es war,
Kam Prinz von Solms mit einer Schaar
Liess einen Strick herüber bringen,
Um unseres Wagens Deichsel schlingen;
Durch Flaschenzuges Allgewalt
Zog man uns dann hinüber bald,
Beendet in gegebener Weise
War damit unsere lange Reise.

Das Lager auf der Zinkenburg, wo jetzt die katholische Kirsche steht, 1845.

Am hohen Ufer, Zelt an Zelt,
In langen Reihen aufgestellt,
Der Raum umzäumt mit Pallisaden,
Zu schützen vor Gefahr und Schaden.
Ein Eingang nur, und der bewacht
Durch einen Posten, Tag und Nacht;
Zum Ueberflusz in zwei Bastionen
Auch noch geladene Kanonen,
Dann noch des Prinzen Kompagnie,
In Stiefeln bis weit übers Knie,
Und Uniformen dunkelgrauen,
Recht schmuck und stattlich anzuschauen.
Der Federbusch am breiten Hut
Stand den beblousten Reitern gut,
Bespornt, die Schwerter an den Seiten,
Iust wie zu Gustav Adolfs Zeiten
Und diese schmucke Reiterei
Manöverierte frank und frei
Auf ihren Merikaner Rossen,
Nach Scheiben wurde auch geschossen.
Zur Sicherheit war das genug,
Und Vorsicht gute Früchte trug,
Wir blieben ungestört in Frieden,
Obgleich die Wilden uns nicht mieden.

Der Häuptling Castro ein Lippan,
Bot gleich dem Prinzen Freundschaft an,
Kam ihn im Lager zu besuchen,
Trank Wein und ass vom deutschen Kuchen.
Mit ihm hat damals Prinz Durchlaucht
Die Friedenspfeife schlau geraucht,
Es war gewiss zu unserm Besten,
Dass Er verkehrt mit solchen Gästen.
Oft waren drauszen wir im Wald,
Erschreckte uns wohl die Gestalt
Von irgend einem Delawaren,
Mit Falkenblick und schwarzen Haaren,
Ein Wink der Hand für uns, ein Grusz,
Fort huschte er mit leichtem Fusz.
Wir, die Erschreckten, lachten heiter
Und gingen unseres Weges weiter.
Im Lager stand das Magazien,
Es war nicht immer viel darin,
Drum fand manch kerngesunder Magen
Gelegenheit, sich zu beklagen.
Oft diente Erbsenbrei statt Mehl,
Ich mache daraus gar kein Hehl,
Für unverdorbene Geschmäcker
Ist Erbsenbrod besonders lecker.
Man mag mir's glauben, jene Zeit
Bracht manche Unannehmlichkeit,
Zum Beispiel, die da mit dem Essen,
Wenn Mundvorrath wurd karg gemessen.
Fleisch gabs genug, wenn nicht vom Rind,
So schosz man einen Hirsch geschwind,
Holt sich auch wohl 'nen Puterbraten,
Das waren keine Heldenthaten.
Es herrschte darum öfter Noth,
Ein jeder sehnte sich nach Brod,
Und hätten wir so gern wie's Leben,
Für Brod, die Braten hingegeben.

Dann war einmal vorbei das Leid,
Ein Wagen brachte Welschgetreid'
Von allen Enden, allen Ecken,
Kam man herbei mit groszen Säcken;
Das Theilergebnisz, leider klein,
Ein Tropfen nur auf heissem Stein,
Drum konnt die Freud nicht lange währen,
Ob der gefaszten vierzig Aehren.
Viel Hunde sind des Hasen Tod,
Gleich gab es wieder neue Noth,
Es war auf Hügeln und in Gründen,
Nur eine Müle da zu finden.
Ein solches Werk, heut unbekannt,
Wurd dann gedreht durch Menschenhand.
Mit Säcken zog man hin in Schaaren,
Um sich den Vortritt zu bewahren;
Oft Morgens, nach durchwachter Nacht,
Hat man sein Mehl nach Haus gebracht.
Zum Schlusse muszte Holz man hacken,
Eh Mutter Kuchen konnte backen,
Doch dann gab's einen Hochgenusz,
Wenn auch nicht grad zum Ueberflusz.
Der Kuchen war gerecht zerschnitten,
So wurde nicht darum gestritten;
Gab es gar Kaffee noch dabei,
Hielt man es für'ne Schwelgerei.
Viel mehr kount ja der Mensch nicht hoffen,
Und wenig blieb zu wünschen offen.

Die erste Ansiedelung der Stadt Neu Braunfels, 1845.

Da Zink die Stadt vermessen hatt',
Fand die Verlosung endlich statt.
Nachher war Mancher nicht zufrieden
Mit dem, was ihm durch's Loos beschieden,

Gerieth in einen wilden Zorn,
Sprach Unvernünstiges verworrn,
Verkaufte schieszlich dann im Dusel,
Den Bauplatsz für'ne Flasche Fusel.
Wer kounte, baute sich ein Haus
Und zog als bald vom Lager aus.
Die Andern mussten es entgelten,
Die noch verblieben in den Zelten.
Sturm mit Gewitter jeden Tag,
Manch morsches Zelt zusammenbrach,
Man hörte jammern in der Pause
Des Regenfalls und Sturmgebrause.
War es gleich nachher wieder hell,
Vergasz man seine Leiden schnell,
Ging wacker an das Klötze spalten,
Ein Obdach daraus zu gestalten.
An jedem Tag es meist geschah,
Dass man ein neues Häuschen sah,
War'n es auch keine Prachtgebäude,
Man hatte daran seine Freude.
Absonderlich wurd oft gebaut,
Wie man es heute nimmer schaut,
Wo jedes Obdach wird zum Segen,
Was ist da an der Form gelegen.
Wir waren, wie man sagte, grün,
Vorischtig tastend, nicht zu kühn,
In vielen Dingen unerfahren,
Die wir erlernt in später'n Iahren.
Ein Ding kam uns dabei zu gut,
Wir hatten immer frohen Muth,
Und lieszen uns durch Schicksalstücken,
Nicht leicht aus dem Geleise rücken.
Oft gab schon eine Kleingkeit,
Uns Grund zu groszer Heiterkeit.
Wir sassen eines Tag's beim Essen;
Ein Indianer unterdessen

Schlich Katzengleich zu uns heran
Und sah die Speisen lüstern an,
Flink hat er dann 'nen guten Bissen
Von Bruders Gabel fortgerissen,
Glückselig schmunzelnd wie ein Kind
Das einen Apfel sich gewinnt.
Wir haben ihm noch mehr gegeben,
Als Lohn für sein energisch Streben.
Ein reizend Bild man später sah,
Es war ein alter Tonqueva
Im Modefrack und mit Cylinder,
Wir freuten uns darob nicht minder.
Der Alte schritt, mit Blicken stolz,
So kerzengrad wie Schindelholz,
Er schien zu wandeln wie auf Rosen,
Es fehlten leider ihm die Hosen.

APPENDIX A.

Letter of Friedrich Ernst to Mr. Schwarz, Oldenburg, 1832.

(From G. G. Benjamin's "Germans in Texas.")

Dear Friend:—

In February of the previous year we embarked on a brig to New Orleans. It was still winter on our departure from New York, then mild spring breezes blew upon us four days after our departure. Between Cuba and Florida we had later real summer, and the whole sea voyage of a thousand miles over that part of the ocean, through the Bahama Islands, into the Gulf of Mexico, up to the mouth of the Mississippi, we lay constantly against the wind and came somewhat back. On the Mississippi up to New Orleans, 120 miles (five make a German mile) we received favorable news of Austin's colony in Texas. We embarked again in a schooner of 37 tons and landed after an eight-day voyage at Harrisburg, in this colony. Each immigrant who wishes to engage in farming receives a league of land; a single person, one-quarter of a league. A league is a league long and the same distance in width. He has in fees for surveying, cost of introduction, etc., to pay $160 in installments; he must take the oath of citizenship and is, after a period of a year, a citizen of the free United States of Mexico; also, as Europeans, who are especially welcome, we received a peculiarly good league of land, and built upon it.

The State of Texas, in which our colony (Austin's colony) makes nearly the sixth part (?), lies in the south (ought to be western coast) of the Gulf of Mexico, between the twenty-seventh degree and the thirty-first degree north latitude (25 degrees 50 minutes to 36 degrees 30 minutes north latitude is the correct latitude), in which also Napoleon's followers have settled. The rivers Trinidad, Rio Brassos (Brazos) and Rio Colorado flow through Austin's colony. It contains the chief city, San Felipe de Austin, and the settlements of Harrisburgh, Brassoria (Brazoria) and Matagardo (Matagorda). One sails in three or four days to Tampico and Vera Cruz. The ground is hilly and alternates with forest and natural grass plains. Various kinds of trees. Climate like that of Sicily. The soil needs no fertilizer. Almost constant east wind. No winter, almost like March in Germany. Bees, birds and butterflies the whole winter through. A cow with her calf costs $10. For ploughing oxen are used. Planters who have 700 head of cattle are common. Principal products: Tobacco, rice, indigo (grows wild), sweet potatoes, melons of an especial goodness, watermelons, wheat, rye, vegetables of all kinds; peaches in great quantity grow wild in the woods; mulberries, many kinds of walnuts, wild plums, persimmons, sweet as honey; wine in great quantity, but not of a particular taste; honey is found chiefly in hollow trees. Birds of all kinds, from pelicans to humming birds. Wild prey, such as deer, bears, raccoons, wild turkeys, geese, partridges (the latter as large as domestic fowls), etc., in quantity. Free hunting and fishing. Wild horses and buffalo in hordes; wolves, but of a feeble kind; also panthers and leopards, of which there is no danger; rich game, delicious roasts. Meadows with the most charming flowers. Many snakes, also rattlesnakes; each planter knows safe means against them. A league of land contains 4440 acres of land, mountain and valley, woods and meadows, cut through by brooks. Through many settlers at one point, the value of it rises so high in price that it has already come to be sold at a dollar per acre. English the ruling speech. Slavery forbidden, but silently allowed. Day labor three-quarters to a dollar, with board.

Clothing and shoes very dear. Each settler builds himself a block-house. The more children, the better for easy field labor. The same manner of life as in North America. Mosquitoes and gnats only common on the coast. Formerly no, and later on only community taxes. Yearly scarcely three months work. No need for money, free exercise of religion, and the best markets for all products at the Mexican harbors; up the river there is much silver, but there are still Indian races there. We men satisfy ourselves with hunting and horse races. On account of the better markets, many people have come here from Missouri. One should go from Bremen to New Orleans; from there to Harrisburg, the cost being $10 per person; goods must be paid extra; children only cost half price; living utensils are bought in New Orleans; with favorable winds the journey lasts only four days. On account of the yellow fever, one should arrive in New Orleans some weeks before the month of July, or after the first of October. Arrived in Harrisburg wagons with oxen are rented to San Felipe where one reports to the land office; it is a good thing if one speaks English; only enough money is needed as is necessary to purchase a league of land. A father of a family must remember that he receives on his arrival, through the land granted to him, a county (Grafschaft), which will come to be worth in a short time, from $700 to $800, for which it is often sold here. The expenses for the land need not be paid immediately. Many raise the money from their cattle. For my acquaintances and former countrymen I have on my estate a stopping place until they have selected a league of land, which is not done so quickly. Colonel Austin, however, promised recently to take care that German arrivals should be settled immediately. Who is unmarried, will bring a good sensible companion for life with him. He who is married, knows that many children belong to wealth. Arrived at San Felipe, ask for Frederick Ernst at Mill Creek. It is 30 miles from there and you will find me. In New Orleans are purchased good axes for cutting wood of Merchant Martinstein, Rue de Chartres. He is a German, and he will take especial care that you have everything necessary. On the journey to San Felippe you must camp in the open air. You must not lack meal and meat, a pair of good boots and a rifle, as well as a saddle are essential needs. The chief city of Texas is San Antonio on the Rio Del Norte. Your friend, Fritz Ernst.

N. B.—Passports are not necessary. Sons over 17 have like part in the settlement of the land.

APPENDIX B.

A Little German Girl in Early Texas.

By Caroline von Hinueber.

(From "The Quarterly" of the Texas Historical Association.)

When my father came to Texas I was a child of eleven or twelve years. My father's name was Frederich Ernst. He was by profession a bookkeeepr, and emigrated from the duchy of Oldenburg. Shortly after landing in New York he fell in with Mr. Fordtran, a tanner and a countryman of his. A book by a Mr. Duden, setting forth the advantages of the new State of Missouri, had come into their hands, and they determined to settle in that State. While in New Orleans, they heard that every settler who came to Texas with his family would receive a league and labor of land from the Mexican government. This information induced them to abandon their first intention. We set sail for Texas in the schooner *Saltillo* (*Säl-teel'-yo*). Just as we were ready to start, a flatboat with a party of Kentuckians and their dogs hitched to our vessel, the Kentuckians coming aboard and leaving their dogs on the flatboat.

We were almost as uncomfortable as the dogs. The boat was jammed with passengers and their luggage, so that you could hardly find a place on the floor to lie down at night. I firmly believe that a strong wind would have drowned us all. We landed at Harrisburg, which consisted at that time of about five or six log houses, on the 3d of April, 1831. Captain Harris had a sawmill, and there was a store or two, I believe. Here we remained five weeks, while Fordtran went ahead of us and selected a league of land, where now stands the town of Industry.

While on our way to our new home, we stayed in San

Felipe for several days at Whiteside's Tavern. The courthouse was about a mile out of town, and there R. M. Williamson, who was then the alcalde, had his office. I saw him several times while I was here, and remember how I wondered at his crutch and wooden leg. S. F. Austin was in Mexico at the time, and Sam Williams, his private secretary, gave my father a title to land which he had originally picked out for himself. My father had to kiss the Bible and promise, as soon as the priest should arrive, to become a Catholic. People were married by the alcalde also, on the promise that they would have themselves reunited on the arrival of the priest. But no one ever became Catholic, though the priest, Father Muldoon, arrived promptly.

My father was the first German to come to Texas with his family. He wrote a letter to a friend, a Mr. Schwarz, in Oldenburg, which was published in the local newspaper. This brought a number of Germans, with their families, to Texas in 1834.

After we had lived on Fordtran's place for six months, we moved into our own house. This was a miserable little hut, covered with straw and having six sides, which were made out of moss. The roof was by no means waterproof, and we often held an umbrella over our bed when it rained at night, while cows came and ate the moss. Of course we suffered a great deal in winter. My father had tried to build a chimney and fireplace out of logs and clay, but we were afraid to light a fire because of the extreme combustibility of our dwelling. So we had to shiver.

Our shoes gave out, and we had to go barefoot in winter, for we did not know how to make moccasins. Our supply of clothes was also insufficient, and we had no spinning wheel, nor did we know how to spin and weave like the Americans. It was twenty-eight miles to San Felipe, and, besides we had no money. When we could buy things, my first calico dress cost fifty cents per yard.

No one can imagine what a degree of want there was of

the merest necessities of life, and it is difficult for me now to understand how we managed to live and get along under the circumstances. Yet we did so in some way. We were really better supplied than our neighbors with household and farm utensils, but they knew better how to help themselves. Sutherland used his razor for cutting kindling, killing pigs, and cutting leather for moccasins. My mother was once called to a neighbor's house, five miles from us, because one of the little children was very sick. My mother slept on a deer skin, without a pillow, on the floor. In the morning, the lady of the house poured water over my mother's hands and told her to dry her face on her bonnet.

At first we had very little to eat. We ate nothing but corn bread at first. Later we began to raise cowpeas, and afterwards my father made a fine vegetable garden. At first we grated our corn, until father hollowed out a log and we ground it as in a mortar. We had no cooking stove, of course, and baked our bread in the only skillet we possessed. The ripe corn was boiled until it was soft, then grated and baked. The nearest mill was thirty miles off.

The country was very thinly settled. Our three neighbors, Burnett, Dougherty, and Sutherland, lived in a radius of seven miles. San Felipe was twenty-eight miles off, and there were about two houses on the road thither. In consequence, there was no market for anything you could raise, except for cigars and tobacco, which my father was the first in Texas to put on the market. We raised barely what we needed, and we kept it. Around San Felipe, certainly, it was different, and there were some beautiful farms in the vicinity.

Before the war there was a school in Washington, taught by Miss Trest, where the Doughertys sent their daughter, boarding her in the city. Of course we did not patronize it.

We lived in our doorless and windowless six-cornered pavilion about three years.

APPENDIX C.

Organische Statute der Colonization.

(From Handbuch für Auswanderer.)

I. Bedingungen der Annahme.

Art. 1. Um als Mitglied der Colonie aufgenommen zu werden, bedürfen die Einwanderer folgende Urkunden:
1. Einen Geburtsakt.
2. Einen Copulations-Schein, wenn sie verheirathet sind.
3. Ein Moralitäts-Zeugniss ihrer früheren Ortsbehörde.

Art. 2. Bis andere Bestimmungen erfolgen, haben dieselben genügende Mittel nachzuweisen um sowohl die Kosten der Ueberfahrt, als jene des Unterhaltes in der Colonie während der ersten 6 Monate zu decken.

Art. 3. Dieselben haben sich 3 Tage vor der Abreise an dem Einschiffungsorte einzufinden. Nur vermittelst eines Annahme-Zeugnisses ausgestellt von der Administration, werden sie auf den Fahrzeugen des Vereins zugelassen.

Art. 4. Die Kosten der Ueberfahrt zerfallen in 2 Classen: *Ueberfahrt mit Verköstigung, Ueberfahrt ohne Verköstigung.* Auswanderer, welche der letzten Classe sich anschliessen, haben zureichenden Vorrath für einen Zeitraum von 2 Monaten—muthmassliche Dauer der Ueberfahrt—nachzuweisen.

Verbindlichkeiten des Vereins.

Art. 5. Der Verein giebt jedem Familienhaupte, welches nach dessen Colonie in Texas sicht begiebt, von seinem Besitzungen 320 Acres Landes, amerikanisches Maas, ungefähr 500 Morgen deutsche Mässung. Jeder unverheirathete Einwanderer, der wenigstens 17 Jahre zählt, hat Ansprüche auf die Hälfte dieses Quantums.

Im Augenblick der Abreice wird jedem Einwanderer ein provisorischer Erwerbstitel zugestellt, welcher später—nach Ausweis des Art 23—gegen einen definitiven Erwerbstitel ungetauscht wird.

Art. 6. Es enthält dieser provisorische Erwerbstitel die Ordnungs-Nummer, welche das Loos bezeichnet, auf welches dem Einwanderer Eigenthums-Ansprüche zustehen. Die Einweisung in das bewilligte Grundeigenthum geschieht an Ort und Stelle.

Art. 7. Es stellt der Verein unentgeldlich die Transport-Mittel für Familie und Geräthschaften der Einwanderer vom Anlandungsorte nach der Colonie.

Die Fürsorge des Vereins wird—sollte sie es sachdienlich erachten—einen Dampfbootdienst auf den Flüssen herstellen.

Art. 8. Es sorgt der Verein für Nahrung und Unterkunft der Einwanderer vom Landungspunkte bis zur Ankunft in der Colonie. Für letzere findet keine Rückvergütigung statt, wohl aber für erstere.

Art. 9. Um der Einwanderer Existenz zu erleichtern und denselben die Mittel zur Arbeit zu verschaffen, wird der Verein in der Colonie selbst ein Magazin—einen Bazar—eröffnen, welches alle nöthigen Lebensbedürfnisse, alle Acker-und Handwerksgeräthe, die Sämereien und überhaupt alle einer Colonie unentbehrlichen Gegenstände darbietet.

Es sorgt der Verein für das zum Ackerbau nöthige Zugvieh. Alle diese Gegenstände sowohl als das Zugvieh werden dem Einwanderer zu dem Preise geliefert, wie solcher sich in der der Colonie zunächst belegenen Stadt herausstellt.

Art. 10. Natural-Vorschüsse werden denjenigen Einwanderern gewährt werden, welche sich durch Aufführung und Thätigkeit zur Arbeit bei der Colonial-Direction empfohlen haben.

Als Garantie für Rückzahlung dieser gemachten Vorschüsse haften die Besitzungen der Colonisten.

Art. 11. Um das Unterbringen der Ackerbau- und industriellen Erzeugnisse der Colonie zu erleichtern, wird das Comptoir des Vereins diese Produkte für eigene Rechnung und nach dem kostenden Preise kaufen, oder Sorge tragen, sie für Rechnung der Colonisten am Orte selbst oder auswärts gegen eine einfache Commissions-Gebühr von 5 Proc.—die üblichen Umschlags-Kosten nicht eingerechnet—zu verkaufen. Jedenfalls steht es den Colonisten indessen frei, ihre Produkte direkt und nach Gutdünken zu verkaufen.

Art. 12. Bis die Bevölkerung zu der Seelenzahl gediehen ist, um selbst die Kosten eines Gottesdienstes zu bestreiten, stellt ihr der Verein eine Kirche zur Verfügung, in welcher die Religions-Uebungen der verschiedenen Culten, zu denen die Colonisten zählen, gefeiert werden können.

Eine besondere Anordnung wird die Stunden für Abhaltungen dieser Uebungen normiren.

Art. 13. Es wird eine Primär-Schule für die Kinder der Einwanderer ins Leben gerufen. Sie empfangen darin:
1. Religions-Unterricht,
2. Unterricht im Lesen,
3. Unterricht im Schreiben,
4. Rechnen-Unterricht und endlich.
5. Unterricht in der deutschen und englischen Sprache.

Art. 14. Es wird in der Colonie eine ärztliche Hülfs-Anstalt, eine Apotheke und ein Reconvalescenten-Haus errichtet werden.

Art. 15. Es stiftet der Verein eine Spar-Casse in welche die Colonisten ihre Ersparnisse niederlegen können. Sie gewährt 5 Proc. Zinsen.

Auf Vorschlag der Colonial-Direction wird der Verein die Art der Einlegung und Zurückziehung der Einlage-Quoten, das Maximum der einzulegenden Beträge normiren.

Art. 16. Unmittelbar nach Ankunft der ersten Einwanderer wird eine Munizipal-Einrichtung geschaffen, und die Rechtspflege durch Anordnung competenter Gerichte gesichert werden.

Art. 17. Bei Arbeiten, welche der Verein für eigene Rechnung ausführen lässt, wird er die Einwanderer vorzugsweise verwenden.

Ein Beschluss der Direction wird dafür einen Preiss-Tarif festsetzen. Es wird der Lohn in Anweisungen auf die Empfänger lautend ‚ausbezahlt, emittirt in Gefolge des § 8 der Vereins Statuten. Die Casse der Colonial-Direction nimmt diese Anweisungen an Zahlungsstatt an; sie werden auf Verlangen des Inhabers gegen Tratten auf die Colonial-Casse auf 10 Tage Sicht ausgewechselt. Da diese Anweisungen einen Repräsentativ-Gehalt bilden, so werden deren niemals mehr als für einen 2/3 des Capitals der Waaren und des Zuchtviehes Werth emittirt werden.

III. Rechte und Pflichten der Colonisten.

Art. 18. Jeder Colonist verfügt selbständig und frei über seine Zeit und seine Arbeit.

Art. 19. Diejenigen, welche für den Verein zu arbeiten angenommen werden, verpflichten sich ihm zu einer Arbeit, deren Dauer durch die Colonial-Direction nach der Jahreszeit und der Art der Arbeit geregelt ist.

Art. 20. Alle Colonisten sind zur Aufrechthaltung der Ordnung und Sicherheit in der Colonie mitzuwirken verpflichtet.

Eine besondere Vorschrift, entworfen von der Colonial-Direction nach dem Bedürfniss der Colonie, wird die Art dieser Mitwirkung festsetzen.

Art. 21. Die Constitution und die Gesetze von Texas reguliren Rechte und Pflichten der Einwanderer als Bürger der Republik.

Art. 22. Jeder Einwanderer ist verpflichtet, drei auf einander folgende Jahre auf dem ihm überwiesenen Landstrich zu verbleiben, daselbst eine Wohnung zu errichten und 15 Acres Landes zu bebauen und zu umzäunen. Die Kosten der Vermessung der den Colonisten bewilligten Ländereien, sind von denselben zu erstatten.

Art. 23. Ein Verbalprozess constatirt die Besitz-Einweisung in die bewilligten Ländereien zur Ergänzung des provisorischen Rechtstitels, wovon in Art. 5 oben die Rede ist. Drei Jahre nach dieser Besitz-Einweisung werden diese provisorischen Rechtstitel gegen einen definitiven Rechtstitel umgetauscht, welchen die texanische Regierung ertheilt.

Art. 24. Stossen die bewilligten Ländereien auf daran hinfliessende Gewässer so sind die Colonisten verpflichtet einen Durchgangs-Weg zu gestatten, dessen Breite der Ortsgebrauch bestimmt.

Ebenso sind sie verpflichtet, die zum Strassen- und Canal-Bau und zu anderen, das allgemeine Beste anstrebenden Bauten erforderliche Ländereien abzulassen.

Nach Umständen geschehen diese Abtretungen umsonst oder gegen Vergütung. *Umsonst* nämlich, wenn diese Arbeiten in den drei ersten Jahren nach der Besitz-Einweisung und auf nicht angebauten, oder nicht bebauten Ländereien unternommen werden; *gegen Vergütung,* wenn diese Arbeiten nach jenen drei ersten Jahren unternommen werden,

oder wenn sie angebaute oder bebaute Ländereien begreifen. ......
Diese Abtretungen gegen Vergütung haben statt gegen gerechte und vorausgehende Schadloshaltung und gemäss deng esetzlichen Erfordernissen.

Art. 25. Die Veräusserung der bewilligte Ländereien durch die Einwanderer, kann—gemäss besonderer Uebereinkunft—nur erst nach Ablauf eines Zeitraumes von fünf Jahren, vom Tage der Besitz-Anweisung an gerechnet, Platz greifen.

Art. 26. Nichterfüllung der vorbemerkten Bedingungen zieht den Verlust der Rechte der Colonisten auf die ihnen bewilligten Grundstücke und die darauf ruhenden Vortheile und Privilegien nach sich.

Art. 27. Einwanderer, welche aus der Colonie nach Europa zurückzukehren beabsichtigen sollten, werden stets Aufnahme auf den Fahrzeugen des Vereins finden; es werden alsdann die Kosten der Rückfahrt nach demselben Massstabe berechnet wie jene der Hinreise.

Art. 28. Es werden diese Statuten—erforderlichen Falls—der texanischen Regierung zur Genehmigung vorgelegt werden.

Art. 29. Es wird die Colonial-Direction, die einzig und allein das Wohl ihrer Colonisten bei allen ihren Einrichtungen anstrebt, eine Wittwen- und Waisen-Versorgungs-Anstalt in's Leben rufen, sobald die Seelenzahl der Colonie einen voraussichtlich günstigen Erfolg garantirt. Sie wird bei deren Verwaltung die Colonisten selbst betheiligten.

Art. 30. Um den Verkehr des Colonisten mit dem Vaterlande und umgekehrt des letztern mit der Colonie nach Kräften zu erleichtern, wird die Direction ein Post-Sicherheits-Bureau organisiren. Sie wird sich zu diesem Ende mit der Post-Verwaltung der Vereinigten Staaten in Neu-Orleans und mit einem angesehenen Handlungshause daselbst in Beziehung setzten.

Art. 31. Der Verein wird Vorrathshäuser einrichten, worin die Colonisten nach der Erndte ein gewisses unbedeutendes Quantum an Getreide einliefern, und woraus dann bei Misserndten oder bei besondern Unglücksfällen, welche einzelne Familien trifft, die nöthigen Vorräthe, unentgeldlich verabfolgt werden.

APPENDIX D.

Constitution of the Verein.*

General Statut für die Colonial-Niederlassungen des Vereins.

ERSTES CAPITEL.

Verwaltung.

Art. 1. Die Ländereien, nach welchen der Verein die Einwanderung richtet, nehmen den Titel Colonial-Niederlassungen an.
Es wird die General-Versammlung den jeder derselben zu verleihenden Namen bestimmen.

Art. 2. Es werden diese Niederlassungen im Namen des Vereins verwaltet; jede hat eine besondere Verwaltung.
Es besteht die Direction jeder solchen Niederlassung:
1. Aus einem Director und
2. Aus einem Rathe von fünf Personen.

Alle werden von dem Comite der Directoren bestellt. Den Vorsitzz im Directorial-Rathe hat der Director. Im Falle des Absterbens oder des Verhindertseins des Directors rückt der zum voraus durch das Comite der Directoren bestellte Vice-Director interimistisch an dessen Stelle.

Art. 3. Der Colonial-Rath wird zusammengesetzt:
1. Aus einem Seelsorger,
2. Aus einem Arzt,
3. Aus einem Civil-Ingenieur,
4. Aus einem Rechnungsführer, und
5. Aus dem Handels-Agenten des Vereins.

---

*Handbuch, pp. 82-95.

Art. 4. Es ist die Dauer der Functionen der Colonial-Agenten nicht bestimmt; das Comite der Directoren normirt die des Directors; sie kann—je nachdem es das Interesse des Vereins erheischt—abgekürzt oder verlängert werden.

Art. 5. Es sind die Gehalte des Directors und der Agetnen entweder fixe oder proportionelle; Art und Betrag derselben setzt das Comite der Directoren fest.

Art. 6. Der Colonial-Director verwaltet allein die seiner Oberaufsicht anvertraute Niederlassung, ihm liegen alle Verwaltungshandlungen ob. Die Agenten und Angestelllten der Niederlassung stehen unter dessen unmitttelbarer Aufsicht, er setzt sie ab, er setzt sie provisorisch, so wie auch im Falle einer Erledigung, sei es im Administrativ-Dienste, sei es in jenem der Direction, unter der Auflage diese Absetzungen und Ernennungen durch das Comite der Direstoren bestätigen zu lassen.

Er ist verpflichtet den delegirten Director binnen drei Monaten davon in Kenntniss zu setzen.

Art. 7. Der Rechnungsführer verwaltet die Casse, überwacht den Vollzug der Befehle des Directors und contrasignirt alle Acte der Verwaltung. Er ist Secretair des Directorial-Rathes.

Art. 8. Er macht dem Directorial-Rath die Vorschläge und hat bei der Abstimmung darüber berathende Stimme.

Der Secretair des Directorial-Rathes führt ein Register über die Anträge, er bemerkt dabei die Verwerfung oder Annahme derselben.

Es führt überdies die Direction ein Tagebuch über ihre Arbeiten und Amtshandlungen.

Alle drei Monate wird ein summarischer Auszug aus dem Register der Anträge und aus dem Tagebuch der Directoren eingeschickt.

ZWEITES CAPITEL.
Fond-Inventarium.

Art. 9. Der jeder Colonial-Niederlassung bestimmte Fond wird durch die General-Versammlung des Vereins festgesetzt. Es bestimmt der Jahres-Voranschlag die Ausgabe, verglichen mit jedem der muthmasslichen Einnahmen, die in die Colonial-Casse jeder Niederlassung einzuschieszende Summe. Das Comite der Directoren bezeichnet diejenigen finanziellen Anstalten der vereinigten Staaten Nordamerikas, zu welchen die Colonial-Direction sich in Beziehung gesetzt hat.

Art. 10. Um den Verkehr der Ansiedler mit diesen Anstalten zu erleichtern, werden Anweisungen auf den Inhaber lautend geschaffen, gemäss § 8 der Statuten des Vereins. Es werden diese Anweisungen als gangbare Münze angesehen und als solche in den Vereins-Cassen angenommen, oder gegen Tratten auf ein Monat Sicht auf die Centrale-Casse des Vereins in Europa, auf Verlangen des Inhabers umgetauscht.

Art. 11. Alle drei Monate lässt der Colonial-Director eine Aufnahme des Cassenbestandes so wohl, als der Ausgabe anfertigen und in jedem Jahre am 31. December werden alle Rechnungen abgeschlossen. Es wird zu derselben Epoche durch des Directors Fürsorge ein Inventarium über den Vermögenstand jeder Niederlassung aufgenommen.

Im Monat August jedes Jahres entwirft der Colonial-Director einen Voranschlag über Einnahme und Ausgabe der seiner Oberaufsicht anvertrauten Niederlassungen für das folgende Jahr, um denselben der Genehmigung des Directorial-Comites vorzulegen.

Es werden alle diese Urkunden, jede zu ihrer Zeit, dem Comite der Directoren eingesandt.

DRITTES CAPITEL.
Anordnung der Arbeiten.

Art. 12. Unmittelbar nach seiner Ankunft an Ort und Stelle lässt der Director, falls dies nicht schon früher geschehen ist, den Plan der Ländereien aufnehmen, auf welchen die Colonial-Niederlassung zu gründen ist. Es werden diese Ländereien in Loose von 640 Acres eingetheilt; jedes Loos erhält eine Ordnungs-Nummer.

Dem Director liegt es ob, die tauglichste Stelle zur Anlegung einer Stadt und von Dörfern ausfindig zu machen, er besorgt die Verloosung der Bauplätze, nachdem er das Gutachten des Directorial-Comites eingeholt hat.

Er lässt Vertheidigungs-Anstalten aufführen, wie er solche zur Sicherheit der Ansiedler nöthig erachtet.

Art. 13. Es setzt sich der Director, Namens des Vereins in direkte Beziehung zu der Regierung und deren Agenten, bezüglich aller das Colonial-Interesse berührenden Einrichtungen.

VIERTES CAPITEL.
Einweisung der Einwander.

Art. 14. Bei Ankunft der Einwanderer am Landungsplatz werden dieselben unmittelbar der Colonial-Niederlassung zugewiesen; Wagen werden zur Verfügung der Frauen und Kinder gestellt und dienen zugleich zum Transport der Effecten der Einwanderer.

Die Direction wird Fürsorge tragen, vom Anlandungspunkte bis zur Colonie, für Ernährung der Ankömmlinge zu sorgen.

Art. 15. Um den Einwanderern Unterkunft während der Nacht zu verschaffen, werden Zelte aufgeschlagen, bis sie ihre Wohnungen beziehen können.

Art. 16. In der Colonial-Niederlassung angekommen wird jede Familie in den Besitz ihres Ländereien—Looses eingewiesen; die Nummer der Reihenfolge in den Registern des Vereins, unter welcher er ingetragen worden ist, entspricht der Nummer des Looses, welches ihm gehört.

Ein über diese Einweisung aufgenommener Verbalprozess constatirt die Besitz-Einweisung; es giebt derselbe Verbalprozess zugleich an, of durch des Vereins Fürsorge auf das dem Einwanderer überwiesenen Loose Gebäulichkeiten aufgeführt sind.

Art. 17. So weit Zeit und Umstände es erlauben, lässt die Direction Gebäulichkeiten aufführen; es werden diese Gebäulichkeiten nach einem Maasstabe und in der Art ausgeführt, dass ihr Kostenbetrag nicht fl. 60 übersteigt.

Art. 18. Der Taglohn der Arbeiter, welche im Dienste des Vereins in den Colonial-Niederlassungen verdendet werden, wird durch die Direction festgesetzt; es wird dieser Taglohn jede Woche in Anweisungen auf den Empfänger lautend, wovon Art. 10 spricht, oder durch Lieferungen bezahlt.

FUENFTES CAPITEL.

Beziehungen der Ansiedler zu der Direction.

Art. 19. Es verschafft die Direction jedem Ansiedler entweder ein fertig gebautes Haus oder die Materialien zur Aufführung eines solchen; sie giebt ihm die Mittel zur Umzäunung und Anbauung von 15 Acres Landes; so wie die zur landwirthschaftlichen Einrichtung erforderlichen Ochsen, Kühe und Pferde.

Es werden alle diese Lieferungen jedem Ansiedler vorschussweise gemacht.

Art. 20. Jedem Ansiedler wird eine eigene Rechnung in den Registern der Colonial-Direction eröffnet, es werden ihm darin alle Vorschüsse zur Last geschrieben, welche ihm—sei es unter welcher Benennung es immer wolle—

geleistet worden sind. Interessen für das erste Jahr werden ihm keine berechnet.

Die Rückzahlung findet zur Erndtezeit statt oder auch früher, wenn es der Ansiedler so vorziehen sollte; es nimmt die Direction von dem Schuldner Felderzeugnisse nach dem laufenden Preise an Zahlungsstatt an.

Art. 21. Es haftet der Direction für diese Vorschüsse das Eigenthum der Schuldner.

SECHSTES CAPITEL.
Politischer Zustand der Ansiedlungen.

Art. 22. Es sind die Colonial-Niederlassungen so wohl als die Ansiedler den Gesetzen von Texas unterworfen.

Art. 23. Um den Vollzug dieser Gesetze sowohl, als die Unterdrückung von Verbrechen und Vergehen zu sichern, und um zugleich Anstände und *Streitigkeiten*, welche sich zwischen den Ansiedlern untereinander oder zwischen ihnen und dem Vereine erheben könnten, auszugleichen und zu schlichten, wir die Colonial-Direction bei der Regierung die Anstellung von Richtern, die Herstellung compenter Gerichte, Ernennung und Installation einer Local-Behörde, alles entnommen aus dem Personal der Ansiedlung selbst, beantragen.

Art. 24. Die Direction wird es sich angelegen sein lassen, regelmässige Civilstands-Register zu eröffnen, Geburts-, Trau- und Sterb-Register aufzulegen.

Art. 25. Es werden—im allgemeinen Interesse—alle männlichen Ansiedler vom 17. bis 50. Jahre eine Stadt-Miliz bilden, um für die Sicherheit von Personen und Eigenthum zu wachen.

Die Direction überwacht deren Organization den texanischen Gesetzten entsprechend.

Art. 26. Eine Zeitung für Handel und Askerbau, wird—wenn erst die Bevölkerung zahlreich genug ist—alle allgemeinen und Sonder-Interessen der Niederlassung besprechen; sie wird die Ansiedler über ihre Pflichten als Ackerbauer und Bürger aufklären.

SIEBENTES CAPITEL.
Gemeinnützige Anstalten.

Art. 27. Der Verein—unter Fürsorge der Direction—wird öffentliche Anstalten in's Leben rufen, welche das Gemeinwohl bedingt.

Sie werden sich nach der Seelenzahl und dem Bedürfniss der Bevölkerung richten.

Art. 28. Es sind diese Anstalten namentlich:
1. Eine Kirche, in welcher der Simultan-Gottesdienst gefeiert wird, so lange die Bevölkerung nicht zahlreich genug ist, um die Kosten der verschiedenen Culten, zu denen sie zählt zu bestreiten.

    Es wird in dieser Beziehung ein Ordnungs-Statut entworfen von der Colonial-Direction, und bestätigt von der Regierung, die Bedingungen dieser Anordnung festsetzen.
2. Eine oder mehrere Freischulen, wo die Kinder beiderlei Geschlechts eine moralische und religiöse Ausbildung erhalten, es wird ihnen darin Unterricht ertheilt im Lesen, Schreiben, Rechnen, in der deutschen und englischen Sprache.
3. Eine Kranken-Verpflegungs-Anstalt, verbunden mit einer Apotheke. Kranke, die zur Aufnahme gemeldet werden, werden darin unentgeldlich aufgenommen und sollen dort alle mögliche Heil- und Linderungs-Mittel finden.
4. Das Haus der ColonialDirecton, wo der Colonial-Rath seinen Sitz haben wird, wo sich die Archive der Colonial-Niederlassungen und

provisorisch das Civilstands-Bureau der Niederlassung befinden wird.

ACHTES CAPITEL.

Vorkehrungen den Handel betreffend.

Art. 29. Der Verein eröffnet, unter Leitung der Colonial-Direction, ein Magazin oder einen Bazar für alle Verbrauchs-Gegenstände und Arbeitsgeräthschaften, welche das tägliche Bedürfniss der Ansiedler erheischt. Die Direction wird es sich streng angelegen sein lassen, dass ihre Magazine stets die zweckentsprechenden Vorräthe, wie solche das Bedürfniss der Bevölkerung mit sich bringt, darbieten.

Art. 30. Sie erzieht Vieh, um gute Racen herzustellen und den Ansiedlern den erforderlichen Viehstand zu verschaffen.

Die Preise von Waaren und Vieh werden stets im Einklang mit dem Curse des zunächst gelegenen Marktes gehalten werden.

Art. 31. Sie nimmt—sei es auf laufende Rechnung, sei es gegen Baarkauf und nach übereingekommenen Preise —alle Ackerbau und industriellen Erzeugnisse der Ansiedler an.

Es werden die laufenden Rechnungen .jedes Jahr nach der Erndte vorgestellt.

Art. 32. Die nach dem ersten Jahre des Aufenthaltes in der Niederlassung den Ansiedler gemachten Vorschüsse werden mit 5 Proc. verzinset.

Art. 33. Es bezieht die Colonial-Direction alle zum Bedürfnisse ihrer Niederlassungen erforderlichen Waaren entweder direkt aus Deutschland oder aus Amerika; ebenso befördert sie nach der oder jeder anderen Gegend die Ackerbau-Erzeugnisse, welche sie durch Tausch oder Kauf erworben hat.

NEUNTES CAPITEL.
Industrielle Anstalten.

Art. 34. Je nachdem es das Bedürfniss der Niederlassungen mit sich bringt, werden industrielle Anstalten in's Leben gerufen; es setzt die Direction den Wirkungskreis jeder derselben fest und legt dem Comite der Directoren den Plan und die Mittel zur Ausführung vor. Jedenfalls wird jede Niederlassung besitzen:
Eine Fruchtmühle,
Eine Schneidemühle,
Eine Mühle, um die Baumwolle zu reinigen.

Art. 35. Die mit Leitung dieser Anstalten beauftragten Agenten und Angestellten, sind gemäss Art. 6 der Oberaufsicht des Directors unterworfen.

Art. 36. Wenn die Colonial-Direction, nachdem sie das Gutachten des Comites der Directoren eingeholt hat, Srassen und Canäle anlegt, Brücken baut und anders das Gemeinwohl anstrebende Verbesserungen vornimmt, so wird sie nach Art. 24 des Colonial-Statuts, rücksicht der Berechtigung der Ländereien richten.

ZEHNTES CAPITEL.
Verfügungen bezüglich der Ländereien.

Art. 37. Es werden des Vereins Ländereien in der Art eingetheilt; dass diejenigen, welche er nicht umsonst verleiht, zwischen diejenigen zu liegen kommen, welche verliehen und in Anbau genommen sind.

Art. 38. Das Comite der Directoren, auf Vorschlag des Colonial-Directors, setzt den Preis der Ländereien und jenen der Bauplätze der Städte und Dörfer, die Art der Zahlung, die Bedingungen der Verkäufe und den Zeitpunkt, wann dieselbe beginnen sollen, fest.

Art. 39. Es finden die Verkäufe im Namen des Vereins durch den Colonial-Director statt, es werden die dessfälligen Urkunden durch den Rechnungsführer contrasignirt.

ELFTES CAPITEL.
Allgemeine Verfügungen.

Art. 40. Wenn der Verein mehrere Niederlassungen begründet hat, wird er einen General-Commissair bestellen und diesen mit der Controlle aller Niederlassungen und mit jener der Wirksamkeit jeder einzelnen beauftragen.

Art. 41. Es werden vorstehenden Bestimmungen alle nöthig erachtete Verbesserungen, nach Genehmigung des Comites der Directoren, hinzugefügt werden.

Petition of Count Carl von Castell to the Duke of Nassau.
(A. D. No. St. M. 2674.)

Dem Herren Grafen Carl von Castell zu Mainz wird auf sein bei seiner Durchlaucht dem Herzog, eingereichtes Gesuch um Genehmigung der Bildung einer Gesellschaft, welche den Zweck hat, den in den Freistatt Texas einwandernden Deutschen Hülfe und Schutz zu gewähren, eröffnet, dass Seine Herzogliche Durchlaucht weder bei der Bildung dieser Gesellschaft noch bei deren Versammlung im Herzogthum etwas zu errinern gefunden, und die Genehmigung deshalb gerne ertheilt haben.

Wiesbaden, den 3. Mai, 1844.
Herzoglich Nassauisches Staats Ministerium.

In Auftrag des Staats-Ministers der Ministerial Referendar:

unterz: Geheimrath, Vollpracht.
Vrt: Stein.

APPENDIX E.

*Aus "Ein Handbuch für deutsche Auswanderer." Bremen,
1846, pp. 63 ff.*

Ueber den Verein zum Schutze deutscher Einwanderer in Texas.

Im Frühling des Jahres 1844 brachten die öffentlichen Blätter nachfolgende Bekanntmachung:

Ein Verein hat sich gebildet, dessen Zweck es ist, die deutsche Auswanderung so viel als möglich nach einem einzigen, günstig gelegenen Punkte hinzuleiten, die Auswanderer auf der weiten Reise und in der neuen Heimath zu unterstützen und nach Kräften dahin zu wirken, dass ihnen jenseits des Meeres eine neue Heimath gesichert werde.

Der Verein erlässt diese Bekanntmachung nicht in der Absicht, Geldkräfte für sein Unternehmen zu gewinnen; das Geschäfts-Kapital ist bereits vollständig gezeichnet. Allein im Bewusstsein des guten Zweckes ist er es dem Publikum und sich selbst schuldig, die Gründe, welche den Verein in's Leben gerufen, die Art und Weise, wie er seine Aufgabe zu lösen hofft und die Grundsätze, die ihn dabei leiten, offen darzulegen.

Der Verein will den Trieb zur Auswanderung weder anregen, noch entschuldigen. Genug, das Bedürfniss besteht einmal, und lässt sich leider eben so wenig wegläugnen, als es möglich ist, jenem immer lebendigeren Triebe Einhalt zu thun. Vielfältige Ursachen wirken dabei zusammen; die Verdrängung der Handarbeit durch das Maschinenwesen, die grossen, fast periodischen Unfälle, die den Handel heimsuchen, die zunehmende Verarmung, eine Folge der Uebervölkerung und des Mangels an Arbeit; endlich wohl auch der gerühmte Reichthum des Bodens im neuen Lande und die manchmal belohnte, oft getäuschte Hoffnung auf ein besseres Seyn und Wirken jenseits der Meere. Unter solchen Verhältnissen müssten die Auswanderer in der That einem besseren Loose entgegen gehen, wenn sie, in wohlgeordneter Masse zusammenhaltend, eine richtige Leitung und einen wirksamen Schutz in der Fremde fänden. Und somit ist die Nothwendigkeit, wie der Zweck des Vereins von selbst gegeben: er will es versuchen, die Auswanderung zu regeln, und zu leiten, damit die Möglichkeit gegeben werde, dass die Deutschen in Amerika eine deutsche Heimath wiederfinden, und aus dem ununterbrochenen Zusammenhange unter sich und mit dem alten Vaterlande ein gewerblicher und Handelsverkehr entstehe, der beiden zum materiellen und geistigen Gewinn gereichen muss. Auf diese Weise wünscht der Verein das Seinige zu thun zu Deutschlands Ehre und Wohl beizutragen, um vielleicht den deutschen Armen eine belohnende Thätigkeit, dem deutschen Gewerbfleiss neue Märkte, dem deutschen Seehandel eine weitere Ausdehnung dereinst zu eröffnen.

Nach langer, sorgfältiger Prüfung hat sich der Verein dafür entschieden, dass Texas dasjenige Land ist, welches dem deutschen Auswanderer am besten zusagen möchte. Das gesunde Clima, die Fruchtbarkeit des Bodens, der Reichthum seiner Ergeugnisse und die Leichtigkeit der Verbindungen mit Europa haben schon seit längerer Zeit eine grosse Zahl von auswanderungslustigen Deutschen dahin gezogen, die jedoch, ohne Schutz und Schirm, sich vereinzelten, und leider oft ganz zu Grunde gingen. Um so mehr musste sich die Aufmerksamkeit des Vereins nach diesen Gegenden wenden. Durch erfahrene und des Landes kundige Männer hat er das texanische Gebiet bereisen lassen, und so vollständige Aufschlüsse erhalten, dass er mit gutem Gewissen und voller Ueberzeugung seine Wahl treffen konnte.

Der Verein hat im gesundesten Theile jenes Landes ein zusammenhängendes noch unbebautes Gebiet von beträchtlichem Umfang erworben, wird dort die Ansiedlung derjenigen Deutschen die das alte Vaterland verlassen, nach Kräften befördern, und hierzu die von den Verhältnissen gebotenen, zweckdienstlichsten Mittel anwenden. Vor dem Abgang wird jedem Auswanderer eine Strecke gutes Landes schriftlich zugesichert, welches er bei seiner Ankunft als Geschenk, ohne alle jetzige oder künftige Vergütung, vom Vereine erhält. Dieser Boden, dessen grösserer oder geringerer Flächenraum sich nach der Grösse der Familie richtet, wird freies Eigenthum des Auswanderers, sobald er drei Jahre lang auf seinem Gute gewohnt. Aber auch vor Ablauf dieser drei Jahre gehören ihm die Erzeugnisse seines Bodens, und der Verein macht weder auf jene, noch auf diesen den geringsten Anspruch.

Der Verein ist ferner dafür bemüht, gute und geräumige Schiffe für die Ueberfahrt auszuwählen; er sorgt dafür, dass es an gesunder, wohlfeiler Nahrung nicht fehle, und die Reisekosten so gering als möglich ausfallen. An den Landungsplätzen sind besondere Agenten damit beauftragt, den Auswanderern mit Rath und That an die Hand zu gehen; die Letzeren finden hier Wagen bereit, die sie mit ihrer Habe unentgeldlich an den Ort ihrer Ansiedlung führen. Auch für ihre Bedürfnisse unterweges wird Vorsorge getroffen. So wie sie an Ort und Stelle anlangen, wird jeder Familie ein eigenes Haus eingeräumt, versteht sich, nur nach dortiger Art aus aufeinander gelegten Balken gezimmert; Vorrathshäuser mit Lebensmitteln, Werkzeugen für Garten und Ackerbau, Samen und Pflanzen aller Art wohl versehen, sichern ihnen Alles, was sie zur Arbeit und zum Leben bedürfen; ebenso finden sie die nöthigen Hausthiere, als Pflugochsen, Pferde, Kühe, Schweine, Schafe, schon an Ort und Stelle. Alles dies wird ihnen zu einem viel geringeren Preise verkauft, als die nämlichen Gegenstände auf den nächstgelegenen Märkten zu haben sind. Solche Auswanderer, deren Betragen und Thätigkeit sich besonders bewährt, erhalten von Seiten der Verwaltung

Vorschüsse, die von der ersten Ernte zurückzuzahlen sind.

Den Auswanderern steht es frei, die Erzeugnisse ihres Ackerbaues und ihrer Gewerbsthätigkeit an die Magazine des Vereins zu veräussern.

Für sittliche und religiöse Erziehung der Kinder zu sorgen, betrachtet der Verein als eine heilige Pflicht; er wird daher, je nach den Bedürfnissen der Bevölkerung, Kirchen und Schulen in der Kolonie errichten lassen. Er wird nicht minder für die Anstellung von Aerzten und Apothekern, so wie für Gründung eines Krankenhauses Sorge tragen.

Eine Gemeindeverfassung und eine Gerichtsordnung, beide nach dem Vorbilde der in Texas anerkannten englischen, werden, sobald es nur thunlich, durch die Verwaltung der Ansiedlungen hergestellt.

Sollten sich unter den Auswandereren einzelne zur Rückkehr nach Europa bewogen finden, so wird ihnen die Heimfahrt zu den nämlichen Preisen, wie die Hinfahrt, auf den Schiffen des Vereins zugesichert.

Der erste Zug von Auswanderern geht im September dieses Jahres 1844 ab; allein schon im Mai werden zwei Mitglieder des Vereins nach Texas reisen, umdort Vorbereitungen zur Aufnahme der Auswanderer zu treffen und die Verwaltung der Ansiedelungen vorläufig einzurichten.

Der Verein wird drei Prozent seiner Einnahme dazu verwenden, um dürftigen Auswanderern die Ueberfahrt und Ansiedelung zu erleichtern. Vorläufig jedoch und bis er diese Absicht zu wirklichen im Stande ist, kann die Niederlassung in der Kolonie nur Denjenigen zugestanden werden, welche die unumgänglich erforderlichen Geldmittel besitzen.

Der unverheirathete Einwanderer bedarf wenigstens ein Capital von 300 Gulden.

Das Haupt einer nicht zahlreichen Familie ein Capital von 600 Gulden.

Um aber auch einer wenn gleich nur kleinen Anzahl von ärmeren Familien sogleich die Ansiedelung möglich zu machen, wird der Verein—in dem er glaubt, den edlen Gesinnungen, die man ihm bereits zu erkennen gegeben, dadurch am besten entgegen zu kommen—eine Liste zu freiwilliger Unterzeichnung eröffnen, deren Ertrag ausscliesslich zu diesem Zwecke bestimmt ist. Jährlich sollen sodann die Beiträge und deren Verwendung, so wie die Namen der Wohlthäter in den gelesensten Blättern Deutschlands bekannt gemacht werden.

Wenn der Verein auf diese Weise, so viel in seinen Kräften steht, dem Unternehmen einen glücklichen Erfolg zu sichern bemüht ist, so beruht doch das Gelingen am meisten auf der ernsten unverdrossenen Thätigkeit der Auswanderer selbst. Das neue Vaterland jenseits des Oceans wird nur dann gedeihlich emporblühen, wenn die Deutschen auch dort sich bewähren, wie sie stets in der Heimath waren: arbeitsam, beharrlich, treu der guten Sitte und dem Gesetze. Darf der Verein auch hieran nicht zweifeln, si wird er doch, um nicht das Wohl und Wehe deutscher Landsleute den Zufälligkeiten eines Versuches preiszugeben, im Laufe dieses Jahres für erste nur ein Hundert und fünfzig Familien zur Uebersiedelung zulassen, und erst dann, wenn diese eine wohlgesicherte Niederlassung gegründet haben, einer weitern Auswanderung mit Rath und That anhanden gehen.

Genauere Aufschlüsse und Auskunft jeder Art werden auf frankirte briefliche Anfragen ertheilt:

Zu Mainz bei der Verwaltung des Vereins zum Schutze deutscher Einwanderer in Texas.

Zu Frankfurt a. M. bei Hrn. *L. H. Flersheim*, Banquier des Vereins.

Gefertigt durch den leitenden Ausschuss des Vereins.

Mainz, den 9. April 1844.

(gez.) *Fürst zu Leiningen.*
In Verhinderung des Grafen Carl zu Castell:
Graf zu Isenburg-Meerholz.